With Liberty and Justice

The Fifty-Day Journey from Egypt to Sinai

Senator Joe Lieberman
with Rabbi Ari D. Kahn

WITH
LIBERTY
AND
JUSTICE

**The Fifty-Day
Journey
from Egypt
to Sinai**

The Samson Family Edition

Maggid Books and OU Press

With Liberty and Justice
The Fifty-Day Journey from Egypt to Sinai

First Edition, 2018

Maggid Books
An imprint of Koren Publishers Jerusalem Ltd.
POB 8531, New Milford, CT 06776-8531, USA
& POB 4044, Jerusalem 9104001, Israel
www.maggidbooks.com

OU Press
An imprint of the Orthodox Union
11 Broadway, New York, NY 10004
www.oupress.org

© Joseph Lieberman 2018

The publication of this book was made possible
through the generous support of *Torah Education in Israel.*

ISBN 978-1-59264-501-5, *hardcover*

A CIP catalogue record for this title is
available from the British Library

Printed and bound in the United States

This sefer is dedicated in loving memory
and in commemoration of the twenty-eighth, כ"ח, yahrzeit of

Julius L. Samson, Esq.
יהונתן בן אליהו מנחם הלוי

*whose exemplary character,
boundless love of learning Torah,
and awe and love of the Law
continue to guide and inspire us every day*

כה אמר ה' עשו משפט וצדקה
"Thus says the Lord: Execute justice and righteousness"
(Jer. 22:3)

Dedicated by

Lee and Anne, A"H, Samson

January 2018 / Shevat 5778

To Hadassah Freilich Lieberman
my love and life partner

And from both of us to our children
Matt, Becca, Jacob, Ethan, Ariela, Hani, and Daniel
and grandchildren
Tess, Willie, Maddy, Camilla, Eden, Yitz, Yoav,
Akiva, Binyamin, Meir, and Avraham Shmuel

with the prayer and faith that they will work for and
enjoy liberty and justice throughout their lives

Contents

SECTION TWO
THE LAW BEFORE SINAI

SECTION THREE
THE TEN COMMANDMENTS

SECTION FOUR

THE LAW SINCE SINAI

SECTION FIVE
SHAVUOT, CELEBRATING THE LAW

Introduction

Passover, the Festival of Freedom, is by far the most widely observed of the Jewish holidays, with the Passover Seder, held on the first night of the holiday, particularly popular with Jews of all backgrounds and denominations.

Shavuot, the Festival of Receiving the Law, which occurs just seven weeks later, is the least observed of Jewish holidays. Many Jews, and most non-Jews, are unaware of Shavuot's existence, though it celebrates a formative experience in Jewish and world history: the Giving of the Law at Mount Sinai. The values reflected in this Law, particularly in the Ten Commandments, have had enormous influence on civilization ever since.

Despite this discrepancy, however, Passover and Shavuot are bound together. In fact, the holiday of Passover is "completed" with the observance of Shavuot, which, with no designated calendar date in the Torah, is determined by the count of days and weeks from the second day of Passover.

The Passover story, in which God hears the cries of the Children of Israel from their slavery in Egypt and reenters history to liberate them, teaches us that freedom is the God-given birthright of everyone. But the Bible also makes clear that the Israelites were not emancipated merely to be free. They were emancipated in order to serve God by accepting and obeying the Law given by God at Mount Sinai, agreeing to live by the values of the Ten Commandments, and disseminating those values throughout the world. This mission has shaped the Jewish people as a nation and defined its eternal destiny. And this understanding explains why observing Passover without following through to Shavuot is at best a half step.

The Bible does not actually describe the fifty days between the two festivals as a journey from slavery to freedom to law. The biblical account of Shavuot is purely agricultural. The Israelites were commanded to bring a grain offering – an Omer – to the Temple on the second day of Passover, in gratitude to God for the first harvest. They were also commanded to count forty-nine days until Shavuot, when they would bring the first harvested fruits – *bikkurim* – to the Temple.

Two millennia ago, after the Second Temple was destroyed and the Jewish people were forced into exile, the rabbis were determined that the important message of Shavuot not be lost. They decreed that the counting of the days connecting Passover and Shavuot be retained even though the Omer offering could no longer be brought to the Temple in Jerusalem. Each of these forty-nine days would continue to be noted, counted, and experienced, as another step on the path from Egyptian slavery to the Law on Mount Sinai. The idea was meaningful and inspired, but the holiday of Shavuot itself never caught on as did its sister holiday, Passover.

Human nature, however, continues to prove the importance of appreciating and observing Shavuot. History has taught us that the freedom God granted on Passover will inevitably lead to chaos, violence, and immorality without the law and the values God presented on Shavuot. People need standards in order to secure, improve, and enjoy their lives. Every society has learned that truth over time.

The annual progression from Passover to Shavuot is a perfect time to remind ourselves that the tension between freedom and law is an ongoing challenge to each of us and to the societies in which we live. But it is this challenge of striking a balance between two "goods," freedom and law, that will produce justice. Americans in particular appreciate the importance of uniting these values, as is clear from our national Pledge of Allegiance to "one nation, under God, with liberty and justice for all."

My purpose in writing this book is twofold: first, to inspire more people to appreciate the necessity and importance of law in our lives, and second, to encourage more people to appreciate and observe the Festival of Shavuot. This holiday, which celebrates the Divine Revelation at Sinai, signifies for a large swathe of humanity – including Christians and Muslims – the dawn of justice.

This book is organized as a substantive supplement to the daily counting of the Omer. It comprises fifty short essays about the Revelation at Sinai and the Law, including the biblical concept of law prior to the Revelation. I hope you will begin reading the first of the essays with the traditional counting of the Omer, on the second night of Passover, and continue to read an essay a day until Shavuot. Of course, when and how you read the essays is up to you. You may read them at your own pace or decide to wait to discuss some of them with friends at a Shavuot learning group. Today, a growing number of Jewish communities around the world convene study groups on the night of Shavuot, in a festival of Torah learning that continues until first light, when morning prayers are said and the Ten Commandments are read. In recent years, some communities in America and Israel have organized Shavuot Torah-study groups across denominational lines. To my mind, this is a perfect way to celebrate Shavuot, and a fitting reminder that the Torah, the Law in its broadest sense, belongs to each and every individual who chooses to accept it. By opening the doors of the study hall to one and all – religious or secular, Orthodox, Conservative, Reform, or Reconstructionist, Jewish, or not – we acknowledge that the Law and its values enable us to live and grow together. While our different forms of worship or observance keep us from praying together, we can study the Law together. Shavuot is a wonderful time to do so.

I am once again grateful to Rabbi Menachem Genack, my teacher and friend, for encouraging me to write this book. Rabbi Genack is the rabbinic administrator of the Orthodox Union and the general editor of the OU Press. I also want to thank Rabbi Genack for introducing me to Rabbi Ari D. Kahn of Bar-Ilan University in Israel. My discussions with Rabbi Kahn, a gifted scholar and writer, together with his suggestions and questions, have informed and improved this book, but I accept full, personal responsibility for everything written in it.

I also want to thank the devoted and gifted teams at Koren Publishers and the OU Press, who have done so much to make ours the golden age of Jewish publishing. At Koren, I am grateful to Matthew Miller (publisher), Gila Fine (editor in chief), Tomi Mager and Shira Finson (assistant editors), Shira Koppel (content editor), and Nechama Unterman and Caryn Meltz (proofreaders). At the OU Press, I thank Rabbi Simon Posner (executive editor). A special thank you to Naomi Kahn for help in editing and organizing the manuscript. I also thank Vernell Glover, my executive assistant at Kasowitz, Benson, Torres, for her support throughout the writing and production of this book.

I write as a layperson, not a rabbi, which means I have less authority, but more latitude. Most of all I write as a committed believer in Judaism who loves Shavuot, the Law, and the law.

Joe Lieberman
New York
2018

Section One

Passover, the Journey Begins

Day 1

My Life in the Law

I have spent all of my professional life in the law – proposing and enacting laws as a Connecticut state senator and United States senator, enforcing laws as Connecticut's attorney general, and representing and counseling private clients as a practicing lawyer. It is surely possible that I would have followed the same career path had I been raised in a religion not as "law-centric" as Judaism is, but I think it would have been less likely.

When I was growing up, my parents and my rabbis taught me that our lives are a gift from God, the Creator, and with this gift comes a covenantal obligation – a legal obligation – to serve God by living according to the laws and values that God gave Moses on Mount Sinai.

Of course, you don't have to be a lawyer to serve God according to those laws and values. But if you are raised to believe that law is necessary to create justice and security in society, which gives your own life purpose, it is natural to want to be an active participant in the larger legal system. This was true for me particularly, growing up in America, where the narrative of law and history closely overlaps the Jewish narrative of law and history.

America's Puritan-Pilgrim founders repeatedly emphasized that their mission was to build not just a new country, but a new Jerusalem of freedom and law. These founders were also influenced by Calvinism, which put the Hebrew Bible at the center of their faith. Their fidelity to the ideas of law and justice, as taught in the Bible, are reflected in the constitution they painstakingly crafted. And the ongoing interpretation and application of the constitution through laws adopted by legislators and opinions issued by judges closely parallels the application and interpretation of the Torah and Ten Commandments by the rabbis through the centuries.

My education in Jewish history and law preceded my broader education in general history and law, and surely shaped my decision to become a lawyer. I am certainly not unique in this regard, as evidenced by the disproportionate number of Jews who have been and are lawyers.

When I went to Yale Law School, I was taught to see the law first and foremost as an expression of our values – a reflection of what we consider right and wrong – but also of our aspirations for ourselves and our society. It represents the ideals and goals we have for ourselves and our country, much as the commandments and values of God-given law have done for thousands of years.

We don't always live up to the law, but it provides a standard for behavior. It makes us better than we would otherwise be.

Day 2

The Show Goes On

The longest-ever running show on Broadway is *The Phantom of the Opera*, a polished and engaging musical that explores a wide range of human emotions. It opened in 1988, and continues to play to sellout crowds.

But my family and I – and, I imagine, you and yours – have been performing in a dramatic production with a far longer run. It is the Passover Seder, presented annually for more than three thousand years. Every Passover Eve, all across the world, members of our extended family prepare for their roles as actors, singers, and storytellers. We provide "dinner and a show" as we tell the story of the liberation of the Children of Israel from slavery in Egypt.

Although every nationality and every family makes individual adaptations, and nuances its version of the story, and though each may sing the text to different tunes or anchor the feast with different cuisines, the Passover Seder retains its shared meaning. It is a celebration of God's love for humanity and humanity's God-given right to be free.

Passover was not ordained to be a singular, isolated moment in our national calendar. It is part of a cycle. The Exodus was the key with which our potential as a nation was unlocked – but what followed was the doorway to realizing that potential.

Every year, for over three thousand years, Jews have counted the days and weeks that lead from Passover, the Festival of Liberation, to Shavuot, the Festival of the Giving of the Law. Passover is only the first act in the drama. Unfortunately, despite the appeal and success of the Passover "production," most people do not remain for the second act: Shavuot. They leave the theater, as it were, before the entire story has been told, missing the point of the annual journey from slavery in Egypt to the Law at Sinai.

The Israelites were not simply released from bondage to be free in the desert. They were not freed to be absorbed into Egyptian society. Their liberation had a purpose, already expressed in Moses' first conversation with Pharaoh: "Thus said the Lord, the God of Israel: 'Let My people go, that they may hold a feast unto Me in the wilderness'" (Ex. 5:1). Later, Moses repeatedly transmits God's request to Pharaoh: "Let My people go that they may serve Me" (9:1).

As the Israelites would soon learn, the purpose of the Exodus was for them to serve God's values by observing God's laws. Their ultimate destination was the Holy Land of Israel, but their first stop was Sinai, where they would receive the Law, and, with it, their national objective and destiny.

In this, the Israelites were unusual. Their national purpose preceded their territorial existence – their values were conferred before their homeland – because the Revelation at Sinai provided the Children of Israel with the values they, and all the world, needed to build a new kind of just society.

Passover and Shavuot are two acts in the same drama whose plot explores how liberty and law must be joined to create justice. The immoral pre-diluvian society of Noah, and the years of Pharaoh's cruel rule in Egypt, demonstrated what happens when people enjoy liberty without law.

Without law, freedom cannot guarantee anyone a secure or good life. That is the point of the second act, Shavuot, in which the rest of the story unfolds, as you will see, if you stay in your seat and experience it.

Day 3

Our Open-Door Policy

As anyone who has ever attended a Passover Seder knows, one of the key sections of the Haggada is built around the give-and-take with four virtual children. One of them is described as the "Wicked Son."

I would like to argue that the "Wicked Son" is not really wicked and that the question he asks – "What is the meaning of this service to you?" – is exactly the kind of question we should be asking each other in our discussions on our journey from Egypt to Sinai.

What is so evil about this query? The rabbis explain that in choosing "you" over "us," this child separates himself from the community and from Judaism and is thus "wicked." To me, though, this is the question of someone who has come to the table to learn.

I believe that this child is trying to understand not just what is happening but what it means and what lessons we can take with us from the Seder. That is not "wicked." That, in contemporary terminology of our hi-tech economy, is disruptive. He is a challenger. But his question – if respected – can, in fact, make everyone at the Seder table better, and earns him the title of the "Challenging Son." This child cares enough about Judaism to come to the Seder. He returns, metaphorically, every year, and is welcomed back by his family, friends, and community. That is a very important lesson for us today.

Too often, we focus on the things that divide us. We define ourselves religiously, by our denomination; politically, by our party; ethnically, by our tribe. One of the main virtues of the Passover Seder is that even those who claim to be outside our community, those who would never pray in *our* synagogue or perhaps any synagogue, make the effort to show up and be part of the conversation. The welcome presence of even the most vocal challengers makes a dramatic and hopeful point: we remain – despite our divisions – one people, united by a shared history, shared values, and a shared vision of a better future.

That is certainly also true of the celebration of Shavuot. We may not all pray together, but we can study the Law and its values together, imbibing this spirit of genuine inclusiveness and the willingness to ask questions as incisive and important as the one posed by the "Challenging Son."

Day 4

Good Debates Produce Good Laws

D ebate is a time-honored Jewish tradition. Hopefully, we will engage in it as we journey through the Omer together. The Talmud itself is a collection of debates, disagreements, and resolutions. Through argument, our ideas are refined, honed, and ultimately strengthened. The following talmudic anecdote about what happened to R. Yoḥanan, the head of the Academy, when his friend and study partner, Resh Lakish, himself a great scholar, died, poignantly illustrates this point:

> Resh Lakish died, and R. Yoḥanan was plunged into deep grief. Said the rabbis: "Who shall go to ease his mind? Let R. Elazar b. Pedat go; his teachings are very sharp." So [R. Elazar b. Pedat] went and sat before [R. Yoḥanan], and on every dictum uttered by R. Yoḥanan, [R. Elazar b. Pedat] observed: "There is a teaching which supports you."

"Are you like the son of Lakish?" complained [R. Yoḥanan]. "When I stated a law, the son of Lakish used to raise twenty-four objections, to which I gave twenty-four answers, which consequently led to a fuller comprehension of the law; while you say, a *baraita* has been taught which supports you! Do I not know myself that my rulings are correct!?" Thus he went on, rending his garments and weeping: "Where are you, son of Lakish, where are you, son of Lakish!" And he cried thus until he lost his mind. Thereupon the other rabbis prayed [that God have mercy] on him, and he died. (Bava Metzia 84a)

R. Yoḥanan had no use for a partner who was simply a "yes-man." He longed for the constant challenges posed by the "adversarial" Resh Lakish, who forced him to step outside the comfort zone of his own certainty, to see things from a different point of view and to reexamine his own ideas through a more critical lens.

As we study the Law, we must remember the value of hearing opinions that differ from our own. By opening ourselves up to reconsidering them from another point of view, we may bring our own ideas and values into sharper focus – or maybe even revise them. Such is the spirit of respectful debate and discussion that I hope to animate through the essays in this book.

This principle is important, not only in studying the Ten Commandments and the Bible, but – and I can tell you this from personal experience – it is critical for those involved in making laws and running governments, as well. People of different ideologies and political parties increasingly argue without listening to each other. They deprive themselves and their ideas of the challenges that can strengthen them and the laws they enact. The result is that too many elected leaders and lawmakers in modern democracies like America have become unable to discuss, negotiate, and compromise. They thus limit their abilities to adopt laws that make the government work, help their constituents, and advance the values of their countries.

Day 5

Go and Learn

The most famous debaters in the Talmud are Hillel and Shammai and their students, and their best-known difference of opinion is this one:

> A non-Jew approached Shammai and said to him: "I will convert [to Judaism] on the condition that you teach me the entire Torah while I stand on one foot." Shammai pushed him aside with the measuring stick that was in his hand. [The non-Jew] then came to Hillel [with the same condition], and Hillel converted him, saying: "That which is despicable to you, do not do to your fellow. This is the entire Torah; the rest is commentary. Go and learn." (Shabbat 31a)

It seems easy for the reader of this story to pick sides. Naturally, most of us prefer the welcoming reaching out of Hillel to the disrespectful harshness of Shammai. Hillel condensed the entire Torah, all its traditions, laws, and values, into one precept. While there are those who might highlight the complexity of Judaism, the myriad rules and regulations, the norms and taboos that have developed over the centuries, Hillel saw past all the detail and formulated a substantive but succinct summary, encapsulating Judaism's guiding principle: "Don't do to others what you don't want them to do to you."

Most people familiar with the story don't notice, however, or remember, that there was more to Hillel's response. It concluded with this additional phrase: "The rest is commentary. *Go and learn.*" In other words, the Golden Rule may be the essence of the "entire Torah," but it is just the beginning. With that foundation, you have a lot more to learn.

"Go and learn" has been a Jewish standard for millennia. We have learned, and we have taught. However, today, too many seem satisfied with the first half of Hillel's message, and fail to accept the proactive mission contained in the second half. After accepting Hillel's wise and embracing opinion, we must also understand the responsibility he placed upon the convert – and all of us – when he instructed him to go and learn so he could gain a full understanding of the Ten Commandments, and the rest of the Torah, and their values. I hope that we will all be motivated to "go and learn," to discover more and more knowledge, to uncover the depth of interpretation of the Torah, on our own or in ongoing conversation with others.

Day 6

Shammai Revisited

We have discussed the importance of debate with people of differing points of view. With that in mind, I feel obliged to ask: Was Shammai's response to the prospective convert really as unreasonable as it appears?

Would a law professor today look kindly on someone who had never studied law, and then asked to be taught the entire jurisprudential corpus in one sentence? Who was Shammai? We know that his personal motto, recorded in the *Ethics of the Fathers*, was "Greet all people with pleasantness." Clearly, Shammai was not as unapproachable and cantankerous a rabbi as his response to the convert suggests. In this case, though, Shammai lost his temper. He was angered by the question. Perhaps he felt that it belittled Jewish law itself. Shammai, we read, pushed the man away – with his builder's measure – in what may be a symbolic action with a crucial message: If you wish to build a sound and worthy legal system, you must first establish a strong foundation. A building with a weak base will eventually collapse.

But why didn't Shammai take the time and effort to explain to the man why his question was simplistic and offensive? That response might have convinced the would-be convert that Judaism is a treasure trove of moral, legal, and philosophical thought that simply cannot be summarized in one sentence. In the final analysis, therefore, I prefer Hillel's response, but I can see some reason in what Shammai did. Judaism should be studied and explored, not leapt over in a single bound.

Various talmudic passages recount how Hillel believed in an "open-door" educational policy: anyone and everyone who wished to study was invited into the Academy. Shammai, on the other hand, set standards for admission. He felt that the Academy should accept only the most gifted.

Both debaters were concerned with Jewish scholarship, Jewish practice, and the future of the Jewish people. The approaches of both to the study of the Law were well reasoned and principled. But each had a distinct approach. Shammai believed that Torah study required rigorous and systematic acquisition of the fundamentals by the most capable students as a foundation for further scholarship. The more democratic Hillel felt that anyone who wished should be afforded access to a Torah education. Both educational philosophies are valid – even indispensable. Education has been at its best when it has allowed both approaches to flourish side by side, creating universal access to education while fostering excellence among the most capable students.

The miracle of Jewish survival is explained, in part, by the capacity of the Jewish people to transmit both laws and values through the parallel systems of education represented by Hillel and Shammai.

Day 7

Repairing the World

If you ask a rabbi today to summarize the essence of Judaism in one sentence, the answer will probably not be Hillel's Golden Rule of "That which is despicable to you, do not do to your fellow." The more likely response would be the Hebrew words "*tikkun olam*," usually translated as "repairing or improving the world."

In the *Aleinu* prayer, source of the words "*tikkun olam*," this phrase is followed by the words "*bemalkhut Shaddai*," or "under the kingship (or sovereignty) of God." In other words, *tikkun olam* is not a rootless, free-floating morality. On the contrary, it evinces a morality grounded in God's clear expression of how we should behave. In much the same way, the Ten Commandments begin with a dramatic affirmation of our faith in God who gave them. The concept of *tikkun olam* presumes that the world and all of us in it need improvement, and it is our responsibility to effect it according to the laws and values God gave at Sinai.

In the Mishna, the first recording of rabbinic law, the concept of *tikkun olam* refers less to ethical or moral considerations and more to a requirement to adopt a macro, and not micro, perspective in making decisions.

For example, freeing a person who has been kidnapped is an extremely important mitzva – a good and righteous deed. Nonetheless, the Mishna insists that one should not overpay to free the hostage, because overpaying to free a hostage would encourage crime, and though the individual who has been set free will be happy, the world would not be a safer place.[1] Criminals would learn that crime does pay. This ancient "macro" application of *tikkun olam* is still relevant to our world today. In adopting laws, we must try to understand their direct and indirect consequences.

In the closing sentence of his 1961 Inaugural Address, President John F. Kennedy summarized the theological-political values of *tikkun olam* – those I had been taught by my parents and rabbis – with the following memorable words:

> With a good conscience our only sure reward, with history the final judge of our deeds, let us go forth to lead the land we love, asking His blessing and His help, but knowing that here on Earth[,] God's work must truly be our own.

These ideas inspired me and many others of my generation into lives of public service and lawmaking, and still do. Each of us, as individuals and as members of society, has the capacity and responsibility to do *tikkun olam*. Enacting good laws and creating good governments is one of the most important ways we can do it.

---

1. See Gittin 45a.

Day 8

Human and Civil Rights

During the summer of 1963, I was one of hundreds of thousands who attended the March on Washington for Jobs and Freedom, which ended at the Lincoln Memorial with Dr. Martin Luther King's "I Have a Dream" speech, one of the greatest orations of my time, or any other. The participants in that march were diverse – racially and religiously – in good part, I believe, because Dr. King placed the struggle for civil rights in the context of broadly shared religious values and religious narratives, including, of course, God's liberation of the Israelites from slavery in Egypt.

Inspired by Dr. King, I traveled with other college students to Mississippi during the fall that year to participate in a Freedom Vote campaign. After I returned to Yale, I heard that Dr. King was coming to Bridgeport, Connecticut, to speak at a rally. Of course, I went.

Dr. King was running a little late, so someone asked me to tell the crowd about what I had seen and done in Mississippi. When I concluded my remarks and began to walk off the stage, Dr. King walked on.

He shook my hand and said in his extraordinary, resonant voice, "Very good, young man." My first thought was that the voice I had just heard was like the voice of Moses – strong, calm, and encouraging. In twentieth-century America, it was.

During my time in the civil rights movement, I was struck that so many of the African American civil rights leaders I met were clergymen and women. I was moved by the way they told and retold the biblical story of the Exodus to inspire and give hope to African Americans fighting for their freedom. For that generation of African American religious leaders, redemption was a national ideal of achieving freedom and justice through law, and not just an inner personal belief related to freedom from sin, as it was for many Jews and Christians. The biblical account of the Israelites' liberation from Egypt instilled hope born of faith, and it ultimately led to the kind of redemption-through-law that the Israelites experienced at Sinai.

Dr. King once astutely reflected: "It may be true that the law cannot make a man love me, but it can stop him from lynching me and I think that's important." It is difficult to think of a historic experience that illustrates more poignantly the singular need for laws to prohibit immoral and unjust behavior in society than America's history of slavery and racial segregation. We needed laws not just to stop lynching, but also to provide equal rights and opportunities in housing, employment, education, voting, and every other area of life in civilized society. But Dr. King was right: no law can itself compel someone to love you if they otherwise hate you.

I got involved in the civil rights movement, and later in the women's rights and gay rights movements, because of my belief that if the religious, ethical monotheism I hold dear means anything, it must be that we are all children of the same God and therefore entitled to equal rights under the law.

That was the promise America's founders made in their Declaration of Independence. Every person is created equal and endowed, not by the government but by God, with equal rights to life, liberty, and the pursuit of happiness. When the Declaration and Constitution were adopted, nothing remotely resembling that equality applied to African Americans, most of whom were then slaves and remained such for decades.

It took almost two terrible centuries of African American slavery and segregation, and then a long struggle in the streets, courts, and legislatures before racial segregation was prohibited by law, and equality of opportunity was mandated. This long and difficult path brings to mind another of Dr. King's iconic statements of faith: "The arc of the moral universe is long, but it bends toward justice." I agree, but the arc bends only if well-intentioned, brave people move it toward justice, usually by enacting and implementing new laws.

That is what finally happened in America during the 1960s, and for women and gay and lesbian and disabled Americans in the decades after – justice through law.

Day 9

Pushing the Limits of the Law

Let's return to Dr. King's statement that "the law cannot make a man love me." That, of course, is true, but in my career as a lawyer, lawmaker, and law enforcer, I have been surprised and impressed by the way in which laws have, over time, changed people's attitudes. For example, after the civil rights laws that prohibited racial discrimination in education, voting, housing, and employment were enacted, many white people, for the first time, lived, worked, and went to school alongside black people. As social science studies have shown, it is more difficult to hate a person you know. It is difficult to maintain a bigotry-sustaining stereotype of a group after you get to know individuals from the group who belie the stereotype. This type of "cognitive dissonance," as described by social psychologist Leon Festinger, demands some social change.

That is what happened over time after the civil rights laws were adopted. The interracial interactions that followed did reduce the ignorance that had bred hatred and bias, and paved the way toward more genuine respect and affection across racial lines in America.

Another extraordinary consequence of legal equality for African Americans was its effect on other disenfranchised groups in America. Once slavery and segregation were challenged through legislation, equality came more quickly to other groups, such as women, disabled Americans, and gay and lesbian Americans. The movement for African American civil rights opened the hearts of the American people and their legislators (and judges) to granting equal rights to other groups of people who, until then, had been marginalized. The remarkably swift acceptance of equal rights for gay and lesbian citizens in recent years resulted, in part, from the cumulative effect of earlier movements and changes.

I believe, as well, that my own political career was influenced by the growing intolerance for discrimination of any kind in America. The confidence that Vice President Gore displayed when he asked me to be his running mate in the presidential election of 2000, making me the first Jewish American to be given such an opportunity, was certainly strengthened by the increased openness of mind and heart that followed the civil rights revolution in America.

When, on the morning of August 7, 2000, the Gore campaign leaked the news that I would be the candidate's running mate, I received a congratulatory call at my home in New Haven from Rev. Jesse Jackson Jr. As I recall it, he said, "Senator, I am excited about your selection because I know you will be a great vice president. But I am also excited because I know that, in America, when a barrier is broken for one group, the doors of opportunity open wider for every other American. This is not only a great day for Jewish Americans. It is also a great day for African Americans."

Eight years later, on the floor of the US Senate, I congratulated Barack Obama on securing the Democratic nomination for president. Thanking me, he surprised me by saying, "I believe that one of the reasons

I have been able to do what I have done so far this year is the way you did what you did in 2000."

I remain grateful for those generous words, as I am heartened by my hope that the adoption of good laws will continue to bring about good changes in social attitudes and behaviors.

Section Two
The Law Before Sinai

Day 10

Paradise Lost and Found

God-given law has been an essential element of human existence since Creation, long before the Ten Commandments were given at Sinai. In fact, the first evidence of a code of "rights and wrongs" can be found in the Garden of Eden.

Eden, a Hebrew word for pleasure, was indeed a place of pure delight, but not of pure freedom. Among the trees of the garden, whose fruits could be enjoyed, were also, as the Bible describes, those whose fruits were forbidden:

> And Almighty God took the man, and placed him in the Garden of Eden to cultivate it and to guard it. And the Almighty commanded the man, saying, "Of every tree of the garden you may freely eat, but of the Tree of Knowledge of Good and Evil you shall not eat, for on the day that you eat of it you shall surely die." (Gen. 2:15–17)

As Adam and Eve were soon to learn, when they were banished from this paradise, disobedience to the divine rules in the Garden of Eden carried severe consequences.

Life in the Garden of Eden also engendered responsibility, as described in the Book of Genesis: "The Lord God took the man, and placed him in the Garden of Eden to cultivate [or enjoy] it and to guard [or protect] it" (Gen. 2:15).

With these words, God instructs Adam and all his future progeny that we have a dual responsibility as the stewards and trustees of His creation – we must work and enjoy His world, but we must also guard and protect it, so that we do not endanger it.

During my long career in public service, environmental protection was a priority for me. Shortly after I was elected to the US Senate in 1988, I convened a meeting with representatives of virtually every national environmental protection organization. One of the environmental leaders at the meeting surprised me by asking why environmental protection was so important to me.

I responded that part of the answer was probably historical coincidence. After all, I had come of age politically in the 1960s and 1970s, when the modern environmental protection movement was born, when the first Earth Day was held, when the first clean air and clean water acts were adopted, and when the federal and state governments created environmental protection agencies. But then I thought some more, and added that the roots of my environmentalism went back much further – all the way, in fact, to the Bible. If you believe, as I do, that the world – including people, animals, plants, air, and water – exists not by accident, but as the result of an intentional act of divine creation, then it is irresponsible not to protect the environment, God's creation, even as we enjoy it.

By the late 1960s, it was clear that we, the inhabitants of God's earth, were not upholding our responsibility to it. Pollutants from businesses, vehicles, and homes were dirtying the air and water, making people sick, shortening lives, and sullying our country's natural beauty. Entire species of animal and plant life were being extinguished as a result of human activity.

As I have noted, the law, while aspiring to the best the community can be, must often limit freedoms in light of the community's greater interests. When realities change, so must the law. During the twentieth century, in the United States and many other countries in the world, national leaders and legislators created a whole new kind of law – environmental protection law – and a whole new generation of governmental agencies to interpret and enforce that law. As a member of the United States Senate Environmental Protection Committee during the 1990s, I had the privilege of participating in the drafting, negotiating, and enacting of bipartisan laws to clean our air and water, preserve endangered species, and protect places of natural beauty.

The great nineteenth-century German rabbi, Samson Raphael Hirsch, spelled out our religious responsibility to all of God's creation in detail:

> The same justice that you owe to man should be shown to every… being, from the earth which bears everything…. Respect all that exists, as God's property…. Respect…all creatures; they are servants in the household of Creation. (*The Nineteen Letters,* Letter Eleven)

The work of protecting the environment goes on – particularly because of growing new threats to it, such as climate change. I am very grateful to have had the opportunity to be involved in the adoption of national environmental laws that have protected the environment and enabled people to live longer, better lives.

Day 11

Law and the Covenant with Abraham

Abraham's history-changing, covenantal relationship with God that is central to Judaism, Christianity, and Islam was characterized by the link between freedom and law:

> And when the sun was going down, a deep sleep fell upon Abram; and, lo, a fear of great darkness fell upon him. And [God] said to Abram, "Know for a certainty that your seed shall be a stranger in a land that is not theirs, and shall serve them; and they shall afflict them four hundred years; and also that nation, whom they shall serve, will I judge; and afterward shall they come out with great wealth. And you shall go to your fathers in peace; you shall be buried in a good old age." (Gen. 15:12–15)

God's promises to Abraham are followed by a sentence that seems out of place: "But in the fourth generation [the Israelites] shall return to this land; for the iniquity of the Emorites is not yet full" (Gen. 15:16).

According to our rabbis' interpretation, the Israelites could not enter the Holy Land until many years had passed, because the Emorites who then lived there did not deserve to be evicted. To the Covenant in which He promised the Land of Israel to Abraham, God attached a clear and unmistakable condition of justice. Thus, Abraham's descendants could inherit the land only when the current inhabitants forfeited their right to it.

This remarkable rabbinical interpretation underscores how divine law is binding on all nations and people. Justice will be served, both on those who lose the land and on those who will inherit it.

This explicit message contains a weighty warning: If the Israelites want to *stay* in the land they have been given by God, they need to obey God's rules and create a just society of laws. For if their behavior is illegal and immoral, the Israelites too will find themselves evicted from the Holy Land, like the Emorites before them. This fear represents a powerful incentive to keep the law and follow the commandments that were given at Sinai.

Today, the Jewish State of Israel cannot be merely the place where most of the citizens are Jewish. Rather, the Jewish state must be defined, as the Jewish people have been since Sinai, as a society in which the values of the Ten Commandments, the fundamentals of justice and the rule of law, are enacted and obeyed.

Day 12

First Choice

The choice of Abraham and his descendants as the torchbearers of the monotheistic covenant with God is much debated in Jewish and other literature. Some say that it was not so much God who chose Abraham as it was Abraham who chose God. While this view is appealing, the Torah itself reveals God's "thoughts," and provides a different answer to the question. As He is about to destroy the evil cities of Sodom and Gomorrah, God explains why He has chosen Abraham:

> God said, "Shall I hide from Abraham what I am going to do? ... For I know him; he will command his children and his household after him, and they will keep the way of God, doing charity and justice." God will then bring about for Abraham everything He promised. (Gen. 18:17–19)

Abraham and his people are chosen because God is confident that they will "keep the way of God, doing charity and justice," or, in other words, obey God's laws. Just a few verses later, when God tells Abraham that he is going to destroy the wicked cities of Sodom and Gomorrah, Abraham proves that God's choice is justified. Instead of quietly accepting God's plan, he argues with God about the morality of collective guilt, and the propriety of destroying an entire city. He questions the justness of the "collateral damage" of destroying the righteous along with the wicked. The Bible records Abraham's heroic challenge:

> And Abraham drew near, and said, "Will You also destroy the righteous with the wicked?... Far be it from You to do such a thing, to slay the righteous with the wicked, [treating] the righteous just as You treat the wicked; far be it from You. Shall not the Judge of all the earth do justice?" (Gen. 18:23–25)

With this stirring monologue, Abraham demonstrates that he was chosen by God because of his faithfulness to the values of the law. This love of justice is the legacy he bequeathed to each of us, teaching us that the "chosen" must live by the law and share the light of the law with the world.

Abraham's powerful words have resonated throughout the ages and always will. When a nation lives by the laws of justice, it can achieve ultimate freedom and peace.

Day 13

Law at the Burning Bush

The connection between freedom and law is clear from God's first conversation with Moses. At the Burning Bush, God tells Moses that He has seen the suffering of the Jewish slaves in Egypt and has heard their cries. He remembers the Covenant, the legal agreement He has made with Abraham, and so will act to liberate the Children of Israel from slavery.

Moses' humble response to God's call elicits a clear declaration by God about why the Israelites would be liberated. This is the Bible's first lesson about the essence of freedom:

> And Moses said to God, "Who am I, that I should go to Pharaoh, and that I should bring forth the people of Israel out of Egypt?" And He said, "Certainly I will be with you; and this shall be a sign to you, that I have sent you: when you have brought forth the people out of Egypt, you shall serve God upon this mountain." (Ex. 3:11–12)

The purpose of the Exodus was not only freedom from slavery. Liberty, despite its luster, was not enough. The purpose of the Exodus was for the Children of Israel to receive God's Law on that mountain – Mount Sinai – and serve God through the injunctions and values given there.

Without the Law they would receive at Sinai, the Israelites would be a fragile, fractious tribe lacking discipline and morality, with a very short national life expectancy. With the Law, this tribe could become a nation, a great nation, defined by the God-given ethical mission expressed in the Ten Commandments.

In His words to Moses, God renews the promise He made to Abraham, Isaac, and Jacob that He would bring their descendants to "a good and large land." But first, they must journey to Sinai, and receive the Ten Commandments. This would enable them to make the land flowing with milk and honey into a truly Holy Land.

At the Burning Bush, God revealed His dual agenda for the mission of the future nation of Israel: liberty and justice. To be truly free, the Israelites would need to build a society of justice with the tools they were to receive at Sinai. The sages of the Mishna eloquently expressed this foundational idea:

> And it says: "And the Tablets [of the Law] were the work of God, and the writing was the writing of God, engraved upon the Tablets" (Ex. 32:16). Read not "engraved" [*harut*] but "liberty" [*herut*], for there is no free individual, except for the one who is occupied with the study of Torah. (Mishna Avot 6:2)

Two millennia later, these words were echoed by Pope Benedict XVI, who said, "When every man lives without law, every man lives without freedom." With the Law given to them at Sinai, as promised to Moses at the Burning Bush, the Israelites would become an eternal and free people with an eternal purpose and destiny.

Day 14

Law and the Waters of Marah

The journey from Egypt to Sinai was short, but it was not easy. First, the Israelites narrowly escaped annihilation at the hands of the Egyptian army. Then, they were attacked from behind by the vicious Amalekites. Afterward, they had to contend with the lack of drinking water:

> They went three days in the wilderness, and found no water. They came to Marah, and they could not drink the waters of Marah, for they were bitter [*marim*]; therefore its name was called Marah. (Ex. 15:22–23)

God came to the rescue and taught Moses how to make the bitter water drinkable. The closing statement of this episode raises interesting questions that are relevant to our focus on law: "There He made for them a statute and ordinance [or judgment]" (Ex. 15:24).[1]

What is the connection between the resolution of the water crisis and the giving of laws? All the people wanted was water they could drink; why add "statute and ordinance" at that time? And what were the statutes they were given?

Rabbi Shlomo Yitzhaki of France (Rashi) explains that the laws given at this juncture were for educational purposes, intended to prepare the people for the actual law-giving that was to follow.

The rabbis believe that the laws taught to the Israelites at Marah – where God purified the water – though not explicitly enumerated, were the laws of honoring parents, the laws of Sabbath observance, and the laws of the red heifer. The red heifer is used to cleanse impurity from a person who has come in contact with the dead. Paradoxically, the heifer renders the person who prepares it impure, while purifying the person who undergoes the ritual.

The first two Marah laws seem to fit in naturally with a pre-Sinai education of the Israelites, but the third is mysterious, counterintuitive, and illogical. What did the laws of the red heifer have to do with the Law the Children of Israel would soon be given as the foundation of society?

Rabbi Yehuda Amital, co-founder (in 1968) of Yeshivat Har Etzion in Israel, was once approached by a group of students involved in Jewish education and outreach, who wished to create an educational program for adults interested in taking their first steps toward Jewish observance. Rabbi Amital suggested that the students take their cue from the three preparatory laws taught by God at Marah. The Torah, he explained, was given to create and strengthen a personal and communal relationship with God. Sabbath observance, which honors God as the Creator, is an excellent place to begin. Our relationship with the law must impact how

---

1. An in-depth discussion of this topic can be found in Rabbi Ari D. Kahn, *Echoes of Eden: Sefer Shmot* (Jerusalem: OU Press/Gefen Publishing House, 2012), 109ff.

we treat one another, as well. Honoring our parents is surely an important first step to good relations with other people that can impact the lives of our children and all those around us.

But our relationship with God often requires a commitment that transcends logic. Divine law sometimes stretches beyond our zone of understanding to elements of religious ritual we would not possibly legislate on our own, no matter how great our desire to benefit our fellows and our society. In Hebrew, this type of law is called "*ḥok*," and it serves as an important test of the faith that precedes law. It is what Kierkegaard called the "leap of faith," and what Rabbi Joseph Soloveitchik called "surrender" to God.

This, I believe, is the point the rabbis are making in suggesting that the enigmatic laws of the red heifer were taught at Marah. It was there that God changed the laws of nature and turned bitter, unpotable water into sweet, drinkable water. That may have been as difficult for the people to understand as some of the laws that followed, but that was, and is, God's way.

Day 15

Unity, Not Uniformity

Dayenu, the title of a favorite Passover Seder song, means "it would have been enough for us" or "we would have been satisfied." The song expresses thanks for the many gifts God gave the Jewish people, each of which, alone, would have been significant, truly miraculous. In one verse we sing, "Had God taken us to Mount Sinai, but not given us the Torah – *dayenu*, it would have been enough." But what would have been the purpose of arriving at Mount Sinai, were it not for the Revelation of the Divine Word and the Giving of the Law there? Did some other noteworthy event happen at Sinai that would have constituted sufficient reason for thanksgiving?

The single family of Jews who had gone to Egypt arrived at Mount Sinai as a much larger tribe, but not yet a nation. At the foot of Mount Sinai, however, they achieved a quality critical to becoming a nation: unity. Commitment to the rule of law unifies a nation – and in fact, after the Law is given, the Israelites together declare: "All that the Lord has spoken we will do" (Ex. 19.8) – but unity is also an important pre-condition for accepting the rule of law in the first place.

The Torah's description of the Israelite encampment at Sinai fortifies this conclusion in a turn of phrase easily lost in English translation. While all the travels and encampments of the Israelites up to this point are described in the Torah in the Hebrew plural, this stop alone is described in the singular:

> In the third month after the Israelites left [plural] Egypt, on the first of the month, they [plural] came to the desert of Sinai. They [plural] had departed from Rephidim and had arrived [plural] in the Sinai Desert, camping [plural] in the wilderness. Israel camped [singular] opposite the mountain. (Ex. 19:1–2)

This sudden grammatical shift leads Rashi, in one of the most moving, inspirational phrases in biblical commentary, to describe the Israelites at this extraordinary moment "as one person with one heart."

A number of other biblical commentators, confirming our assertion above, point out that the unity at the foot of Mount Sinai was a necessary prerequisite to the great Revelation and receiving of the Law. But this extraordinary unity of "one person with one heart" reveals another important aspect of the Revelation. God's presence at Sinai was perceived, understood, and appreciated by each and every Israelite in a unique way, in accordance with his or her own personality, intelligence, and capabilities. Yet, each individual was a critical and indivisible element of the one unified nation.

This individualized, yet unifying, nature of the Revelation – of truth itself – explains why, since Sinai, rabbis have been engaged in an ongoing process of expounding the Torah, applying it to new realities, and answering new questions. It also explains why this process continues to yield so many different opinions and interpretations. These reflect diverse, but legitimate, perceptions of the word of God. All are part of a whole, just as each individual who stood at Sinai was part of one unified whole. That unity was a huge achievement and a great gift in itself, and that is what the *Dayenu* Seder song is teaching us.

Since Sinai, and particularly today, our challenge in religion and in life is to understand that even opinions that are different from our own contain a piece of the divine. We must find within ourselves the love and strength to value and cherish those opinions, as well as the individuals who express them. This, I believe, is the lesson of the wording of the verses leading up to the Revelation as it shifts from plural to singular. Unity made the Revelation at Sinai possible. In every generation, we must work to replicate the unity of Sinai and the mutual respect that prevailed there. Without it, the national purpose of living the Law can never be fully achieved.

Day 16

Seeing the Sounds

Fifty days after the Children of Israel left Egypt and arrived at Mount Sinai, God spoke to them. It was one of the most transformational moments in human history.

In the Bible, the experience itself is described in detail, following the Ten Commandments:

> And all the people saw the sounds, and the lightning, and the sound of the shofar, and the mountain smoking; and when the people saw it, they trembled, and stood far away. And they said to Moses, "Speak with us, and we will hear; but let not God speak with us, lest we die." (Ex. 20:15–16)

The Children of Israel apparently "*saw*," but did not "*hear*," God's voice, and they trembled. They begged Moses to speak to them – instead of God – and only then would they be able to "hear."

The rabbis note other peculiarities in the text surrounding the Revelation. For example, the verse that introduces the Ten Commandments contains a seeming redundancy: "And God spoke all these words, saying" (Ex. 20:1). Sensitive to every word in the Torah, the sages of old were convinced that this construction conveyed a message beyond the literal meaning of the phrases. After all, the verse could simply have read, "God said." Why does it include the word "saying," and why does it need to tell us that God said *all* the words that follow?

Some explain that the primary importance of the encounter at Sinai was the experience; the content was secondary. If so, why would God have chosen to communicate this great body of law and values in a manner that so overwhelmed the senses of the intended audience that they were incapable of hearing and understanding it?

The answer may lie in the difference between seeing and hearing. We can actually see things with greater perspective from a distance, but the quality of what we can hear depends upon how close we are. More importantly, we are capable of seeing a great many sights at one time – details, nuances, patterns, large and small things – but we can usually hear only one utterance at a time.

The rabbinic commentaries describe the uniqueness of the Revelation in terms of the experience shared by the nation assembled at the foot of the mountain. The people saw a broad panorama. God showed them the great canvas, the complex image of the system of personal and communal law that would be their guide and their mandate from that day forward. To make it applicable to human life and society, they needed to hear and internalize, appreciate and analyze the details. But the Children of Israel were overwhelmed by the experience of God's voice. They withdrew, and forfeited the opportunity to hear the details directly from God, opting instead to receive instructions through Moses.

A similar tension exists today. Many people love the broad ethical teachings of Judaism, yet they find the details of observance tedious or outdated. They consider Halakha, "Jewish religious law," to be no more than a collection of technical minutiae. Others love the details, constantly examining and reexamining the applications and implications of Jewish legal principles. In so doing, they sometimes seem to lose sight of the larger picture, of the objective to which this system of law and values aspires. God's Law was designed both to inspire and to guide. The goal of Revelation for our time, as it was at Sinai, is to combine these two visions, the large picture with the small details. Through this synthesis of both aspects of the Law, individuals and nations can become holy.

Day 17

Nahshon, a Leader Who Changed History

I have written earlier about how God – the Creator, the Liberator, the Law Giver – charged humans with the responsibility of working to improve His world by living according to the values of the Ten Commandments and the Bible. God granted us the invaluable gifts of life, liberty, and law; each of us must use these gifts – strengthened by our faith and guided by God's Law – to act, to lead, and to repair the world.

Nowhere is this division of responsibilities between God and humanity seen more clearly than at the Red Sea. As Pharaoh's massive army closes in on the Israelites, trapping them at the water's edge, they panic, as recorded in Exodus 14:

> As Pharaoh came close, the Israelites looked up. They saw the Egyptians marching at their rear, and the people became very frightened. The Israelites cried out to God. They said to Moses,

"Weren't there enough graves in Egypt? Why did you have to bring us out here to die in the wilderness?" (Vv. 11–12)

Moses tries to calm them. He prays to God to save them. The Almighty's response is astonishing:

God said to Moses, "Why are you crying out to Me? Speak to the Israelites, and let them start moving. Raise your staff and extend your hand over the sea. You will split the sea, and the Israelites will be able to cross over on dry land." (Vv. 15–16)

God says here clearly that this is not the time for prayer. It is time for faith-based action by the Israelites bolstered by the truly incredible promise God has just made that Moses will split the sea, and the Israelites will walk through to freedom on the other side.

The Midrash, which records oral traditions that clarify and explain the Torah, tells us that when Moses held up his hand over the Red Sea, *before* the waters parted, Nahshon, the leader of the tribe of Judah, affirmed his faith in God's promise and his understanding of man's responsibility by walking into the sea. He waded further and further in, until the water was as high as his nostrils. Then, and only then – in response to Nahshon's faith and action – did God split the Red Sea.

The salvation of the Israelites at the Red Sea was due to God's miraculous intervention in nature and history, but it did not happen until man took the first step, literally. Moses' guidance and intercession on their behalf and Nahshon's courageous leadership enabled the Israelites to move on to Sinai and receive the Law.

In the generations since those critical moments at the Red Sea, the Law and its values have been sustained and advanced through similar leadership. Each of us has within us the capacity to be Nahshon. Each of us knows that without faith, without leadership, without courage, without taking principled risks in our lives and careers, progress is impossible.

I have found this to be true in politics. It is certainly true in business, and it is also true in the life of every person who aspires to live by
the moral standards of the Ten Commandments.

Section Three

The Ten Commandments

Day 18

The First Commandment: "I am the Lord Your God"

T he magnificent supernatural displays at Mount Sinai before the giving of the Ten Commandments were a fittingly grand overture to the Divine Revelation that was about to take place:

> And Mount Sinai was all enveloped in smoke, for God had descended upon it in fire, and its smoke rose up like the smoke of a furnace, and all the mountain shook. And the sound of the shofar grew louder and louder. Moses spoke and God answered him with a voice. (Ex. 19:18–19)

This is the perfect preface to the First Commandment, which is not so much a commandment as it is a declaration by God that the commandments to follow emanate from Him. God, who created and formed the natural world at His will, and then altered it through the plagues in Egypt, the splitting of the Red Sea, and the awesome lights and sounds at Sinai, was about to change the human world forever – with a new system of laws designed to make the world more just.

There were systems of law before Sinai – but no other began with God. To be effective, a system of law must be credible and legitimate in the eyes of the citizenry. Some never are. Others derive their legitimacy from popular referendum, constitutional convention, or executive fiat. But none has as much legitimacy and credibility as the Ten Commandments and the Bible. They came from God. That is the most significant attribute of the First Commandment; it is the foundation for all that follows.

An exchange between Moses and the Israelites, after the Ten Commandments are given, adds even more purpose to the unnatural phenomena – the sound and light show – witnessed at Sinai. As we discussed above, the people are terrified, and they plead with Moses, "Let God not speak to us, lest we die." Moses reassures them, saying, "Do not be afraid, for it is to uplift you that God comes so, and that His awe may be upon you, that you should not sin" (Ex. 20:16).

In other words, God is an active initiator of a legal system that distinguishes sin from virtue and right from wrong. And He instills the fear and awe of Heaven to teach that He will reward virtue and punish sin.

The way God identifies Himself in the First Commandment is important. He is not, here, the God who created heaven, earth, and humanity, but rather the God "who brought you out of the land of Egypt, out of the slave house" (v. 2).

God prefaces the laws of justice – the nine other commandments – by recalling the prodigious act of justice He has just performed in liberating the Israelites from slavery. By holding up a high and noble standard for human behavior, God turns the First Commandment from a statement of divine self-identification alone into a moral imperative to act. All who accept the commandments are called upon to assure freedom and, more broadly, justice for all.

Day 19

The Second Commandment: "You Shall Have No Other Gods"

In the Second Commandment, God admonishes us that it is not enough to acknowledge that the Ten Commandments are the work of the God who emancipated the Israelites from slavery. We must also believe, with perfect faith, that He is the only God.

That belief takes us back to Creation and reminds us that if there is only one God, then all of us are part of His creation, and therefore inherently brothers and sisters, not just children of different families, tribes, nations, or religions. We are one family with one Father.

From that shared beginning, laws of equal opportunity and equal treatment emerge naturally. The Declaration of Independence, drafted by the leaders of the American colonies to free themselves from the autocratic rule of the British Crown, was based on the self-evident truth that all people are created equal and endowed by their Creator – not by the government – with the same inalienable rights to life, liberty, and the pursuit of happiness. It was to secure those rights, as the brave American founders explained, that they were establishing their new government. All these rights were based on faith in God, our Creator, as expressed best in the Hebrew Bible.

Years ago, when I was at Yale, my rabbi from Stamford asked me if I would invite Yale's famous and controversial chaplain, William Sloane Coffin, to come from New Haven and speak at our synagogue one Friday night. Chaplain Coffin graciously agreed. In his sermon, he offered an additional, more individual interpretation of the Second Commandment, connecting it to the words of God in Deuteronomy chapter 11. These are recited twice daily in the second paragraph of the *Shema Yisrael* affirmation of faith: "Be careful lest your heart be tempted and you go astray and worship other gods" (v. 16).

Chaplain Coffin argued that "other gods" did not mean only idols or other gods. "Other gods" also included ungodly behavior, such as materialism and greed, infidelity, violence, and other actions prohibited by the Ten Commandments. These can become "gods" that some people worship more than God Himself.

Our faith in God as the Creator and as the only God, articulated in the Second Commandment, also obligates us to the moral imperative of "Godly" behavior in all aspects of our lives.

Day 20

The Third Commandment: "Do Not Take the Name of the Lord Your God in Vain"

When I was growing up, I was taught that the Third Commandment meant that we should not ever use God's name in swearing. Many decades and a fair share of swearing later, it still seems wrong to use God's name for that purpose.

But when I became a lawyer, and then a legislator, the Third Commandment took on a different meaning for me. I understood that God's name was invoked in the courtroom oath not in vain, but as the guarantor that a witness in court or before a legislative hearing would tell "the truth, the whole truth, and nothing but the truth, so help me God." Because God is the source of all holiness, when God's name, holy in itself, is invoked to support an oath, the community feels confident that the oath taker will uphold his promise or risk incurring God's wrath.

The most important oaths I myself have taken were on the occasions I was sworn in as a public servant: five times as a state senator, two times as attorney general, and four times as a US senator.

This is the oath I was required to take as I began each new term as a US senator:

> I do solemnly swear that I will support and defend the Constitution of the United States against all enemies, foreign and domestic, that I will bear true faith and allegiance to the same; that I take this obligation freely, without any mental reservation or purpose of evasion, and that I will well and faithfully discharge the duties of the office on which I am about to enter. So help me God.

I made this clear promise to "support and defend the Constitution of the United States" each time I began a term of office, and I made it in God's name, with all the responsibility and accountability therein entailed.

And I made this promise in God's name with my hand on a Hebrew Bible, given to me by my father, Henry Lieberman, who received it, as did every other Jewish soldier serving in the US army during World War II.

Pledging allegiance to the Constitution of the United States always felt comfortable to me, not merely because it upholds individual rights and promotes justice, but also because of the larger historical context in which I was educated. When the Jewish people were forced into exile after the destruction of the First Temple in Jerusalem, the prophet Jeremiah gave them guidelines for conducting themselves in the Diaspora, as a minority within a larger society:

> Thus says the Lord of hosts, the God of Israel, to all who are carried away captives, whom I have caused to be carried away from Jerusalem to Babylon: Build houses, and dwell in them; and plant gardens, and eat their fruit.... And seek the peace of the city

where I have caused you to be carried away captives, and pray to
the Lord for it; for in its peace shall you have peace. (Jer. 29:5–7)

These instructions have served for centuries as a guide for Jews throughout the world: obey the law of the land, and respect the authority of the
law. A short, familiar axiom, which appears in several places in the Talmud, encapsulates this policy: "The law of the land is the law."

Of course, there are exceptions, if the laws of the land in which
we live are inhumane or immoral. The same is true of oaths. If I lived in
a land of tyranny, taking an oath of loyalty to the tyrant in God's name
would itself be a violation of the commandment not to take God's
name in vain.

But I live in, and have served, a country which promises every
citizen equal rights and due process of law. Swearing loyalty to such a
country and its constitution in God's name always felt right and comfortable to me.

Day 21

The Fourth Commandment: "Remember the Sabbath Day to Keep It Holy"

No commandment more clearly illustrates the way in which laws that ostensibly limit our freedom can actually make us more free than the commandment to observe the Sabbath. This Fourth Commandment can be viewed as a paradigm for our journey from Egypt to Sinai, from freedom to law.

A good friend, who is Christian, once joked with me: "I could never be an Orthodox Jew. Too many rules. Too many 'Thou shalt nots.'" It certainly is true that the commandments in the Torah and the rabbis' explications of their proper observance contain a lot of "Thou shalt nots." However, I have increasingly understood that most of those prohibitions are ultimately liberating, not restricting, particularly those regarding the Sabbath.

Rabbi Joseph Soloveitchik wisely observed that Shabbat can indeed be burdensome. After all, the day interrupts our personal autonomy, our ability to do what we wish, when we wish. Shabbat observance therefore requires of man – in Rabbi Soloveitchik's opinion – a certain surrender to God.

For me, that moment of surrender comes on Friday afternoon when the sun is about to set and I know that I have to turn off my smartphone. Modern man has become a slave to the brilliant devices that, in so many ways, have freed us from drudgery and created our extraordinary quality of life. However, cars, phones, computers, and automation in general can be addictive and controlling. Once I disconnect on Friday, once I surrender to God and the Sabbath, it feels great. I am free.

That is one reason why I wrote a book about the Sabbath called *The Gift of Rest.* The prohibitions on the Sabbath give me the gift of a day that is different from the other six days of the week. Free of the responsibilities of work, I can spend more time in prayer, be with my family, rest, or simply enjoy the unique day.

One of the reactions to my book about the Sabbath that I most cherish came from Cecil Samuelson, a leader in the Mormon Church, who was then president of Brigham Young University. He told me that after reading *The Gift of Rest*, he realized that he was allowing his smartphone to interfere with his Sunday Sabbath observance, so he decided to turn it off from late Saturday night until early Monday morning. This created a mild panic on campus when people could not reach him on Sunday, but if they urgently needed him, they knew they could call him or visit at his home. Nonurgent matters would wait until Monday. Thus, freed from unnecessary interruptions, President Samuelson was able to enjoy the blessings of the Sabbath.

Day 22

The Fifth Commandment: "Honor Your Father and Mother"

The Torah tells us that the Ten Commandments were engraved on two tablets of stone:

> And He declared to you His covenant, which He commanded you to perform, the Ten Commandments; and He wrote them upon two tablets of stone. (Deut. 4:12–13)

The traditional assumption from this biblical description has been that the commandments were equally divided between the two tablets, with five engraved on each. In almost all portrayals of these tablets of stone, the right side has the first five commandments, which the rabbis say deal with the relationship between man and God, while the commandments on the left tablet are concerned with relationships between people. But what is the rationale for putting the Fifth Commandment, regarding honoring parents, with the first four commandments relating to the relationship between God and man? The Talmud addresses this question:

> When God said, "I am [the Lord your God...]" and "You shall have no [other gods...]," the nations of the world said, "He is preaching for His own self-aggrandizement." However, when He said, "Honor your father and mother," they acknowledged and praised the first [four commandments as well]. (Kiddushin 31a)

The commandment to honor parents is surely about the interpersonal relations between parents and children. We honor our parents because they brought us into the world. They care for us, love us, give us shelter and sustenance; logically, the least we can do in return is to give them the honor and gratitude they deserve.

The rationale behind the commandment, however, speaks to man's relationship with God. By grouping this commandment together with the other commandments about the man-God relationship, the Torah conveys a profound message. When we understand and internalize the need to honor our parents for all they do for us, we raise a deeper question: Who really brought us into this world? Who really sustains us, and provides us with food and shelter? The answer, of course, is God. In this way, the Fifth Commandment teaches us to channel our innate feelings toward our parents into the strongest foundation for the rule of law – belief in God. This placement of the Fifth Commandment also reminds us that our parents are God's partners in our creation.

The Fifth Commandment includes a frequently overlooked second clause: "so that you may live long in the land that the Almighty your God is giving you" (Ex. 20:11). This second clause singles out the honoring of parents as a good deed that will be rewarded with a long stay in the Promised Land. It is reminiscent of the language from Deuteronomy that appears in the second paragraph of the *Shema Yisrael* prayer, which makes clear that the Israelites' stay in their Holy Land is contingent on their being a holy people and following God's commandments.

Here, in the Fifth Commandment, God elevates the honoring of parents as a value whose embrace by the Israelites will enable them to live long in the Land of Israel. Why? A nation where children honor their parents is more likely to be a nation where the law is honored, and immorality, violence, and disorder are diminished.

Day 23

The Sixth Commandment: "Do Not Murder"

In the preface to his volume on laws regarding murder, Maimonides describes the importance of the Sixth Commandment:

> Although there are other sins that are more serious than murder, they do not present as serious a danger to society as murder does. Even idol worship – and needless to say, sexual sins or the violation of the Sabbath – are not considered as severe as murder, for these other sins involve man's relationship with God, while murder also involves man's relationship with his fellow man.
>
> Whoever commits this sin is an utterly wicked person. All the mitzvot that he performs throughout his lifetime cannot outweigh this sin or save him from judgment. (*Mishneh Torah, Hilkhot Rotze'aḥ UShemirat Nefesh* 4:9)

Some biblical scholars suggest that the way in which the Ten Commandments are presented can help us better understand them. For example, as we saw earlier, the order of the commandments and the division into two groups of five teach us important lessons. Similarly, according to some rabbis, rather than reading each group of five from top to bottom, on each of the two tablets, the commandments should be read horizontally, across both tablets, and linked to each other this way. Thus, the First Commandment should be paired with the Sixth as below:

> I am the Lord your God, who brought you out of the land of Egypt, out of the house of slavery / You shall not murder.

Murder is an egregious crime, as described by Maimonides, and self-evidently wrong, but what is the most significant reason why? When the First and Sixth Commandments are read as one sentence, the primary reason for the prohibition of murder is clear: "I am your God." The reason human life is holy and murder is evil is because every human is created in the image of God.

This reading of the First and Sixth Commandments is supported by the verse in Genesis that first prohibits the spilling of blood, long before the injunction from Sinai: "Whoever sheds man's blood, by man shall his blood be shed; for in the image of God He made man" (Gen. 9:6).

Rabbi Soloveitchik brings a deeper perspective to the consequences of committing murder. He once suggested that the first line of the *Shema* be translated, "Hear O Israel, God (the Eternal) is our Lord, God is unique." He felt that translating the word "*eḥad*" as "one," as it is in most prayer books, misses the point. Of course, Judaism believes in one God. The declaration of the *Shema*, however, is intended to articulate the uniqueness of God. He is unlike anything in our experience. He is beyond our imagination.

According to this interpretation of *Shema*, we can say that just as God is unique, all human beings, created as they are in the divine image, reflect this uniqueness. To kill a human being is to deprive the world of that unique spark of the divine, the particular aspect of God embodied and expressed in that person. Every individual is irreplaceable, because each and every human is part of the mosaic of God's image as it is revealed in this world. This must be what the sages meant when they taught that whoever kills one person destroys an entire world, and whoever saves one life saves an entire world.[1]

This respect for every individual, which underlies the Ten Commandments, should be the foundation of any good legal system. And this sensitivity to the unique sanctity of every human being should inform the laws with which we strive to build just, humane, and moral societies.

---

1. Y. Sanhedrin 4:9.

Day 24

The Seventh Commandment: "Do Not Commit Adultery"

The succinct Seventh Commandment has been applied broadly by the rabbis. "Do not commit adultery" has been interpreted to prohibit any behavior that undermines marriage. Certainly, the commandment prohibits sexual contact with someone other than a spouse, but it has also been interpreted to forbid use of language, in public, which demeans one's spouse or one's marriage.

Such extended applications of the prohibition of adultery are based on the view that marriage is a sacred covenant in which God is the third participant, and upon which so much of the strength, tranquility, and potential of society depends. One of the most interesting expressions of this insight is found in Alexis de Tocqueville's *Democracy in America*. Among his brilliant observations on nineteenth-century America, Tocqueville noted: "There is no country in the world where the Christian religion retains a greater influence over the souls of men than in America."[1]

One of the most significant effects of that religiosity, Tocqueville believed, was the strength of marriages in America, which was at least partially the result of Americans' adherence to the Seventh Commandment. Tocqueville even suggested that the strength of American marriages might be the key to American freedom. "As long as family feeling is kept alive, the opponent of oppression is never alone," he wrote.[2]

The institution of marriage and the definition of family have changed significantly since Tocqueville's time. Fewer people are getting married; the incidence of divorce is much higher; there are many more single-parent families; and same-sex marriage has been legalized in America, and in a growing number of other countries, in recent years. But Tocqueville's basic observation is still correct. Religious observance, including following the commandment that prohibits adultery, continues to be one of the best foundations for strong marriages and good families. And strong families are an important force in building a better, perhaps even a freer, society.

1. Alexis de Tocqueville, *Democracy in America* (New York: Modern Library, 1981), 182.
2. Tocqueville, *Democracy in America*, 182.

Day 25

The Eighth Commandment: "Do Not Steal"

The need to prohibit theft as a precondition of a just society seems obvious. We have seen how, in regard to some of the other commandments that also seem self-evident, the rabbis have interpreted the commandment as a baseline for behaviors and actions not expressly mentioned. The Eighth Commandment prohibition against stealing, likewise, has been interpreted to apply to more than the taking of another's real or personal, tangible property. For example, some rabbis say it refers even to not responding when another person greets you, because that represents theft of the other person's self-worth.

This last argument may seem far-fetched until we consider one of the harmful effects of today's social media. How many unfortunate cases have we heard of in which victims of public slander or internet bullying are so embarrassed and deprived of self-respect that they commit suicide?

Day 25

One group of talmudists wondered about the placement of the prohibition against theft following the commandments against murder and adultery, both of which are punishable by death. They argued that theft, in any fair system of law, could not be punishable by death, and concluded that the Eighth Commandment must be warning against theft of a person – as in kidnapping – in which the victim is sold into slavery. That, the rabbis knew, was a crime punishable by death.[1]

This reasoning may seem dated, and yet it is particularly relevant when we think of the horrific stories we have all heard of trafficking in humans – kidnapping young men and women and selling them into sexual slavery.

Unfortunately, the realities of life require a legal system capable of deterring theft by adapting laws that punish new forms of theft that arise, such as identity theft, computer hacking, internet bullying, and human trafficking.

---

1. Sanhedrin 86a.

Day 26

The Ninth Commandment: "Do Not Testify as a False Witness"

Every child is taught the virtue of telling the truth. In America, one of our best-known national legends is about our first president, George Washington – who, as a boy – had the courage to admit to his parents that it was he who had cut down their cherry tree. Washington's truth telling also protected others – including perhaps one of the family slaves – from being falsely accused of felling the tree and therefore prevented an injustice.

The Ninth Commandment is all about law and justice: "Do not testify as a false witness against your neighbor." Courts cannot achieve their great societal purpose of interpreting, applying, and enforcing the law if the individuals who appear in them do not tell the truth. Undoubtedly, this is why two of the Ten Commandments, this and the

Third, which deals with legal oaths, are devoted to the legal process, as distinguished from the law itself.

In addition, the Talmud, in its many interpretations and examples, teaches that the biblical verse which discusses falsehood – "Distance yourself from false matters" (Ex. 23:7) – relates to courtrooms.[1]

The Talmud takes the requirement for truth in the courtroom so seriously that it prohibits not just outright lies, but also giving false impressions, verbally or non-verbally. For example, the rabbis say that, in the courtroom, one should not stand casually next to a witness for fear that the judge or jurors will infer sympathy with that person's testimony. When testifying, a witness must not withhold any information; suppressing part of the truth fosters a false impression of the truth. It is tantamount to bearing false witness, and stands in the way of justice.

Outside of the legal system, the requirement to tell the truth becomes less absolute. If the truth will hurt someone, and not serve any good purpose, remaining silent can be the moral choice.

The biblical source for this difficult decision is in Leviticus: "Do not go about as a talebearer among your people" (19:16). The rabbis interpreted this verse to mean that it is forbidden to say anything derogatory about another person even if it is true, unless the person you are telling it to has a genuine need to know it. In Hebrew, this type of talk is called "*lashon hara*," which literally means "evil tongue."

The talmudic rabbis (and rabbis since) devoted much thinking and writing to the problem of spreading gossip, truthful or untruthful. Rabbi Joseph Telushkin suggests the reason is that "the biblical commandment forbidding gossip is probably the most widely disobeyed of the 613 laws of the Torah."[2]

In the information age, with billions of people communicating instantly with people they both know and don't know, the prohibition

---

1. Shevuot 30b.
2. Rabbi Joseph Telushkin, *Jewish Literacy* (William Morrow and Company, 1991), 522.

against *lashon hara* is violated more than ever before and the results of those violations are graver than ever. Beyond the personal harm, our societies have become divided and defensive, and our civilization has been coarsened.

From my experience in politics, I can confirm what you already know from having seen TV ads during political campaigns. Candidates spend most of their budgets paying for commercials that attack their opponents. Some of the attacks are totally false; some are partially false or at best misleading; and some are *lashon hara*, truthful, but negative, and providing no information useful to the voters in deciding their vote. All are morally reprehensible.

Most candidates will explain, as I have at times, that they hate to "go negative," but it seems to work and effectively preempts the inevitable attacks of political opponents. Unfortunately, no law can fix this. Here, we have to rely on a candidate's conscience, or his or her "fear of Heaven." It will take more than that to do *tikkun olam* on our political system, but it is definitely way past time that we started trying.

Day 27

The Tenth Commandment: "Do Not Covet Anything Your Neighbor Has"

The Tenth Commandment, because it is divine, goes where no earthly legal system would go. It goes to the source of most of the law-breaking, evil, and immorality on earth. This last commandment aims to get inside our heads and hearts and reduce our desire for what we do not have, thus strengthening our capacity to follow the other commandments. Unlike the statutes of typical human legal systems, which only hope to regulate behavior, the Tenth Commandment sets a higher standard by aiming to regulate the thoughts and desires that precipitate bad behavior.

Envy of another's property precedes theft; envy of another's spouse precedes adultery; envy of another nation's land or power precedes war; envy precedes political corruption; envy even precedes murder. Perhaps the old adage should be adapted to read, "Envy goeth before a fall," because it usually does.

Envy is a natural emotion, and controlling it is difficult. God's laws, like the human legal systems patterned after them, are, as we have discussed, aspirational. They express the way we imperfect humans know we should be and would like to be, but are not quite yet. The laws are hopeful, because they imply that positive change is possible, and more likely, among people governed by a good legal system.

Rabbi Abraham ibn Ezra, the prolific medieval Bible commentator and philosopher, defined the sin of coveting as the illogical desire for something that is, by definition, beyond one's grasp, and cannot be attained. He offered an allegory designed to liberate a person from the desires prohibited by the Tenth Commandment: A person born into the common classes, for example, would not seriously entertain desire for the daughter of the king, or imagine that marriage to her would be possible. He would thus banish any such thoughts from his mind. So too, all individuals should banish from their thoughts desire for possessions beyond their reach.

Today we would take issue with Ibn Ezra's analogy. Are we not encouraged to reject artificial limits on personal achievement? Is not every American boy and girl taught to believe that they can grow up to surpass the achievements of their parents, to become president of the United States (or at least be nominated to run for vice president)? Modern sensibilities chafe at the idea that there are worthy goals that are beyond our reach. If social structure, for example, no longer places the "king's daughter" metaphorically beyond our reach, is the desire itself no longer prohibited? I would say that it is not.

A question regarding real estate transactions was posed to Rabbi Asher Weiss, the head of a rabbinical court and a well-known *posek,* "decisor of religious law," in Jerusalem. The argument involved the prohibition of coveting. In his decision, Rabbi Weiss stated that normal business practices that involve behaviors that might appear as "coveting" are most certainly permitted by Jewish law. For example, the Talmud never prohibited a person from walking into a store, finding an object that he or she desires, and paying the proprietor for it. Coveting, Rabbi Weiss held, is the desire for an object that is not for sale, and the use of unfair, unconventional, inappropriate means to acquire it (Maimonides, *Mishneh Torah, Hilkhot Gezeila VaAveida* 1:9).

As members of consumerist societies, we know that significant industries – marketing and advertising – exist for the sole purpose of arousing within us the desire to acquire things that are not yet our own. If you are engaged in one of these businesses, do not worry that you are automatically breaching the Tenth Commandment. Rabbinical opinions make clear that normative advertising practices in modern commercial settings encourage us to desire things that are attainable, for a price. Hopefully, it is with money we have, or is, at least, within our credit card limit.

The final cautionary word goes to the wise rabbis who wrote the *Ethics of the Fathers*: "Who is rich? He who is happy with his lot" (Mishna Avot 4:1).

Day 28

Upholding the Values of the Ten Commandments

When I was a child, there was a family hour on television devoted to programming for the entire family, that parents would feel comfortable viewing together with their children. That is clearly gone. Today, at any hour, children can watch on TV the values of the commandments being ignored. And, if that's not enough, they have access to any number of other media – movies, music, video games, and of course the internet – that include openly sexual or violent content.

During the 1990s, worried parents in Connecticut turned to me, their senator. They felt defeated by an entertainment culture, which, they feared, was influencing their children far more than they were able to.

I had my voice and the Senate pulpit. I joined with like-minded Democrats and Republicans, including Tipper Gore and Bill Bennett, in arguing that the entertainment culture was adversely affecting the values of our children and therefore of our country. We called on the entertainment industry to self-regulate to protect our children. We introduced legislation that would compel the industry to adopt better content-rating codes. Some media outlets decided to adopt their own improved systems and to offer TV filters for parents who wanted to control the content available to their minor children. Though the Seventh Commandment that prohibits adultery and upholds marriage was never explicitly mentioned in the advocacy or our legislative proposals, its values were clearly under attack.

Then, in the summer of 1998, President Clinton's relationship with White House intern Monica Lewinsky came to light. I was an early and strong supporter of Bill Clinton and proud of all that he was accomplishing as president, so his offensive behavior was truly heartbreaking to me. Now, parents in Connecticut appealed to me to speak out against the president.

I was torn. Certainly, President Clinton's conduct had disparaged his wife and undermined their marriage. But were his actions not his private business? And they didn't seem to affect the high approval ratings he continued to enjoy for the job he was doing as president.

In the end, I decided to speak out because the president of the United States is not privileged with private conduct. The actions of the most powerful person in the country will probably become public and will influence behavior throughout the country. That is especially true today in the age of social media, but it is a lesson taught by the Bible millennia ago. In the Bible, the higher your position, the more demanding the standard to which you are held, because of the greater impact your behavior, good or bad, has. Perhaps that is the reason the kings of Israel were commanded to carry their own Torah scrolls with them at all times. The Torah, not the king, was the last word, and the king would do well to remember that. Moses, the greatest prophet and devoted leader, was denied entrance to the Promised Land because of one lapse of faith. King Saul forfeited his kingship because he failed to execute fully God's stern instructions about how to deal with the Amalekites.

In a speech on the Senate floor on September 3, 1998, I called on the president to accept full responsibility for what he had done and to apologize to the country. I argued that, fair or not, presidents did not have a right to privacy because their private behavior, once publicized, had enormous societal consequences. The speech received much more attention than I expected, mostly because I was the first Democrat to call the president to account. I was surely his first friend and supporter to do so.

A week later, the president convened an interfaith gathering of clergy in the White House, at which he movingly took responsibility for his actions, and asked for forgiveness. The following Sunday morning, he called me at my home and said he agreed with all I had said, and assured me that he was being counseled regularly by two clergymen.

I hope that President Clinton, and all of us, will ultimately be judged by a merciful God, who heeds our contrition and good intentions for the future. In the meantime, each of us must continually strive to realize the values of the Ten Commandments in all aspects of our lives.

Section Four
The Law Since Sinai

Day 29

Interpreting the Commandments

In the Book of Deuteronomy (4:2; 13:1), Moses twice instructs the Israelites and their descendants that they can never add to nor subtract from the words of God that he brought down from Sinai.

But the commandments were general statements of principle given more than three thousand years ago. From the outset, the people needed interpretation and guidance about how to apply them. In the years since, as the world has moved from the agricultural age to the industrial age and, more recently, to the information age, the need to adapt and change is even more acute.

God, and Moses, understood there would be a need for a judicial process that would interpret and apply the law over time, as recorded in the Bible:

If you are unable to reach a decision in a case involving capital punishment, litigation, leprous marks, [or any other case] where there is a dispute in your territorial courts, then you must set out and go up to the place that God will have chosen, and appear before the Levitical priests [and other members of] the supreme court that exists at the time. When you present your case, they will declare a verdict. Since this decision comes from the place that God shall choose, you must scrupulously obey all their instructions to you, carefully following their every decision. [Besides this, in general,] you must keep the Torah as they interpret it for you, and follow the laws that they legislate for you. Do not stray to the right or left from their words. (Deut. 17:8–11)

A process was thereby established for permissible analysis and development of the law by credible authorities. What was prohibited was adding mitzvot, "commandments," and claiming that these were the word of God transmitted at Sinai. Anyone who claims a divine mandate to add to or subtract from the law is, according to the Torah, a false prophet.

An additional basis for ongoing human input into Torah law is found in Leviticus: "You shall safeguard My statutes" (Lev. 18:30). This command became a mandate to "erect a [protective] fence around the Torah" (Mishna Avot 1:1) and establish rules that keep people as far as possible from violating God's commandments and statutes.

The seminal compilation of Jewish oral law known as the Mishna preserved hundreds of years of rabbinic discussions regarding the interpretation of law and the creation of "protective fences," from the early years of the Second Temple until approximately the year 200. These rabbinic discussions were analyzed, supplemented, and reapplied by Torah scholars over the next three hundred years, and resulted in the Talmud, "learning," or Gemara. Both the Mishna and the Talmud were transmitted orally for generations, until the vicissitudes of exile and persecution placed the entire system in jeopardy. Eventually, the Oral Law was transcribed and the rabbis of every generation were entrusted with making contemporary applications of ancient law. This serious subject has been the object of Jewish humor. There is a story of a rabbi of old who had been asked many questions about how to apply a particular provision of the kosher laws. He prays to God for assistance and is shocked to hear the Voice of God (VOG) respond:

> VOG: How can I help you, my dear rabbi?
>
> Rabbi: Almighty God, many of my congregants have asked me about the commandment in Your Law that we should not cook the meat of a calf in the milk of its mother. Does that mean we can never eat meat and milk together?
>
> VOG: You shall not cook the meat of a calf in the milk of its mother.
>
> Rabbi: Does that mean we have to wait hours after we eat meat to eat milk products?
>
> VOG: You shall not cook the meat of a calf in the milk of its mother.
>
> Rabbi: Does that mean we have to have separate milk and meat plates, utensils, pots, and pans?
>
> VOG: (After a pause) OK. Have it your way!

This joke makes an important point. Without the interpretation of the law by scholars and rabbis that began after the destruction of the Temple in Jerusalem, when the Jewish people were forced into exile, the Jewish people might not even have survived to return to

Israel as they did in the last century. And if Ezra and Nehemiah had not stepped forward to lead, legislate, and apply the commandments during the Exile, the Torah would surely not be as vibrant and relevant as it is today.

Interpreting the Constitution

The process of interpreting and applying the laws of the Torah, which continues with tremendous vitality, is mirrored in rule of law societies like America and Israel with regard to civil and criminal law, and with the same life-sustaining results.

When it comes to the reach of law however, the difference between Jewish law, Halakha, and civil and criminal law that I enacted as both state senator and US senator for thirty-four years is enormous. Unlike religious laws, secular laws generally do not aim to regulate every aspect of our personal and private lives – as well they should not.

The limits on law in America were established by our constitution. They grew out of the spirit of independence and individual liberty that animated America's rebellious founders. These limits were further entrenched by the Bill of Rights, which protects personal rights such as freedom of speech and freedom of religion. The system of checks and balances built into the American government has made it the responsibility of the courts to determine whether legislatures or executive agencies have violated the people's liberty, or pushed the law too far into private life.

But, like the Torah scholars who interpret religious law, the judicial branch of the US government continues to interpret the constitution, occasionally finding within it the basis for new rights by applying existing codes to new realities.

One of the best examples of this is the right to privacy, first articulated by Louis D. Brandeis, a Jewish American giant of the law. In 1890, as a Harvard Law School student, Brandeis wrote a *Harvard Law Review* article (together with Samuel Warren) entitled "The Right to Privacy." In it, he bemoaned the unwanted newspaper coverage of people's personal lives. Declaring that the individual had a right to be let alone, Brandeis wrote words that ring true over one hundred years later, in today's social media milieu:

> Instantaneous photographs and newspaper enterprise have invaded the sacred precincts of private and domestic life, and numerous mechanical devices threaten to make good the prediction that "what is whispered in the closet shall be proclaimed from the housetops."

Almost forty years later, in 1928, after Brandeis had become a justice of the United States Supreme Court, he dissented from a majority of his colleagues in *Olmstead v. United States.* This court decision held that wiretapped phone conversations obtained by the government without a judge's approval, and then used as evidence in a criminal prosecution, did not violate the Fourth or Fifth Amendments. Justice Brandeis wrote:

> The makers of our constitution undertook to secure conditions favorable to the pursuit of happiness. They recognized the significance of man's spiritual nature – they sought to protect Americans

in their beliefs, their thoughts, their emotions, and their sensa-tions. They conferred, as against the government, the right to be let alone – the most comprehensive of rights and the right most valued by civilized men.

Almost forty years later, in 1967, after Justice Brandeis had passed away, the Olmstead decision was reversed (in *Katz v. United States*), and Brandeis' position became law.

The process by which the right of privacy was established par-allels the foundational pledge of the rabbis of the Talmud that, while never adding to the commandments given by God at Sinai, they would interpret and apply them to emerging realities. Thus have our secular courts related to the constitution from the outset.

Day 31

Law and Morality

In the Bible, immediately after the Ten Commandments are handed down, God teaches Moses laws about building the sacrificial altar, and then tells him to place ordinances before the Israelites.

Over the centuries, the commentators have explored the significance of this sequence – from the big principles of the Ten Commandments, to the architectural specifications of building the altar, to the details of civil and criminal law. The rabbis draw this primary lesson: God does not want there to be a separation between religion and everyday life, or between ritual obligations and ethical behavior. The profound moral norms of the Ten Commandments and the spirituality of the altar must inform every aspect of how we conduct our lives. In other words, God's Law is meant to be pervasive and to infuse all elements of our existence with holiness. The prophets make clear that God places greater value on ethical social behavior than on strict ritual observance that ignores the needs of others. Isaiah makes this point beautifully:

> When you spread your hands in prayer, I will hide My eyes from you – because your hands are full of blood. Wash yourselves, purify yourselves, remove the evil of your doings from before My eyes.... Learn to do good, seek justice, strengthen the victim, do justice for the orphan, take up the cause of the widow. (Is. 1:15–17)

In general, Scripture repeatedly reminds us what our priorities should be in making this kind of personal judgment, as in I Samuel 15:22: "Has the Lord as great delight in burnt offerings and sacrifices, as in hearkening to the voice of the Lord? Behold, to obey is better than to sacrifice, and to hearken than the fat of rams."

One striking example, taught by Rabbi Joseph Soloveitchik, concerns Yom Kippur, the holiest day in the Jewish calendar.[1] In Temple times, the most important person on this day was the High Priest, who performed the rituals of repentance in the innermost sanctum of the Temple. In preparation for this awesome responsibility, the High Priest was removed from his regular tasks for days; he was even separated from his wife for a full week. However, if the High Priest happened upon a corpse on the eve of Yom Kippur (of a person who, for various reasons, no one else will bury), notwithstanding the prohibition against priests touching a dead body, he would be obligated to defile himself and see to it that the deceased received a dignified burial. In this dramatic example, human dignity triumphs over ritual, even though the beneficiary would never know about the kindness that had been extended to him. In sum, the Law itself allows for exceptions, in circumstances where strict observance would clash with ethical behavior.

---

1. In a lecture delivered January 3, 1958. See Rabbi Ari D. Kahn, *A River Flowed from Eden* (Kodesh Press, 2015), 187.

Day 32

From Sinai to Philadelphia

The Ten Commandments presented a radical departure from the sources and systems of law that preceded Sinai. They also had a profound influence on the systems of law adopted after Sinai.

One of the great differences between the laws of the Hebrew Bible and the laws of other great ancient civilizations like the Chinese and Greek is that in the Hebrew Bible, God is the source of the Law. As the Torah makes clear, what happened at Sinai was totally the result of divine revelation.

As we have discussed, the Law given by God to the Jewish people was accompanied by the responsibility to share it. Early in its history, the Roman Catholic Church embraced the Ten Commandments as divine revelation. Saint Thomas Aquinas said that because no person can know the entire natural law (the belief that certain values and rights are inherent in human nature), God revealed it in the Ten Commandments, so it could be understood by everyone.

In the sixteenth century, Calvin and the Reformation were instrumental in elevating the place of the Hebrew Bible and the Ten Commandments in Protestantism; that, in turn, brought the legal traditions from Sinai directly into the laws of England and then, through the Puritan and Calvinist pilgrims, to America.

The substance and language of America's founding documents echo the Hebrew Bible. The American Declaration of Independence opens with an explanation by the founders that they are breaking their ties to England "to assume among the powers of the earth, the separate and equal station to which the Laws of Nature and of Nature's God entitle them." The authors go on to make clear that, more than an avowal of their right to be politically independent from the British Crown, this Declaration of Independence is a statement of national purpose and values. In it, the nascent United States of America asserts its independence based on several self-evident truths, including that "all men are created equal, that they are endowed by their Creator with certain unalienable Rights, that among these are Life, Liberty, and the pursuit of Happiness." They declared that it was "to secure these rights" that their new government was being formed.

This seminal document of American history and the Ten Commandments are strikingly congruent. As President Kennedy said in his Inaugural Address of 1961, "The same revolutionary beliefs for which our forebears fought are still at issue around the globe – the belief that the rights of man come not from the generosity of the state but from the hand of God."

The long journey from the Revelation at Sinai to the Declaration at Philadelphia put us on the shared path of laws and values that we strive to follow today.

Day 33

From Law to Government

The need for a system of good governance, to ensure security and administer justice, is illustrated in the Bible, even before Mount Sinai, in a conversation between Moses and his father-in-law, Yitro:

> The next day, Moses sat to judge the people, and the people stood around Moses from morning to evening. When Moses' father-in-law saw... he said, "Why are you sitting by yourself and letting the people stand around from morning until evening?"
>
> And Moses replied to his father-in-law, "The people come to me to seek God... they come to me, and I judge between a man and his neighbor and I teach them God's decrees and His laws."
>
> Moses' father-in-law said to him: "What you are doing is not good. You are going to wear yourself out, along with this nation that is with you.... You cannot do it all alone.... I will give you advice and God will be with you: You must seek out from among the people able, God-fearing men, men of truth, who

hate injustice, and appoint them over the people…. Let them administer justice; they must bring every major case to you, but they shall judge every minor case themselves." (Ex. 18:13–24)

In response to Yitro's insights and recommendations, Moses created a judicial system and the beginnings of a federalist government. Everything that happened afterward in the development of law and Jewish nationhood followed those first steps to self-governance.

Although skeptics often claim that governments are created by politicians for the benefit of politicians, the truth is that governments are established, and laws are adopted, and courts and legislatures are organized, by the citizenry, out of necessity. They are the instruments through which people try, at the most basic level, to protect their security, and then, increasingly, to improve the quality of their lives.

Of course, this doesn't mean that every law and judicial interpretation is wise and constructive, or that every governmental agency is necessary. But it does mean that when governments don't exist, people have to create them for their own safety and well-being. As the sages teach in *Ethics of the Fathers*, "Pray for the welfare of the government, for were it not for the awe of it, men would swallow one another alive" (Mishna Avot 3:2).

Nearly a millennium and a half later, Thomas Hobbes echoed this thought. In *Leviathan*, his 1651 landmark treatise of modern political philosophy, he laid out his vision of the natural state of humankind without centralized government, in these words: "…wherein men live without other security, than what their own strength, and their own invention shall furnish them withal…. And the life of man, solitary, poore, nasty, brutish, and short."[1] The American Founding Fathers, as we have seen, ultimately rejected Hobbes' support for absolute power,

---

1. Thomas Hobbes, *Leviathan* (London: Penguin Classics, 1985, 1986, 1987), 186.

and embedded in the Declaration of Independence and the Constitution ways to protect the inalienable rights of individuals and to limit the reach of government.

Day 34

Filling the Gaps in Secular Law

T he men who founded America had mounted a rebellion against the English monarchy, and against the "long train of abuses and usurpations" they had increasingly suffered at the hands of the British king. That is the main reason why they created a government of limited powers and checks and balances.

The framers of the constitution also understood, though, that since their government of limited powers would not try to control every act of every citizen through law or regulation, they would need nongovernmental partners to promote domestic tranquility and morality. No institution was more embraced for this purpose by America's founding generation than religion.

George Washington best reflected this in his advice to future generations of Americans in his memorable Farewell Address, delivered on September 19, 1796:

And let us with caution indulge the supposition that morality can be maintained without religion...reason and experience both forbid us to expect that national morality can prevail in exclusion of religious principle.

In a society of free people, where government would limit its own control, Washington argued, religion is the best non-governmental source of personal accountability and public security.

The greatest religious influence on our American founders came from the Calvinist Protestants who believed in the Hebrew Bible and the Ten Commandments, and therefore appreciated the purposive reach of religious law, as distinguished from secular law, into the private lives of citizens.

This distinction between limited governmental law and expansive religious law may also help explain why America's founders protected freedom of religion in the First Amendment, and declared in Article Six of the Constitution that "no religious test shall ever be required as a qualification to any office or public trust under the United States." Perhaps they included this unprecedented guarantee because they believed that a vibrant religious life in America was an indispensable guarantor of its national morality and destiny.

Day 35

Filling the Gaps in Religious Law

As comprehensive and all-encompassing as the laws emanating from the Bible are, there are behaviors that the Bible does not specifically approve or prohibit and that the rabbis have not addressed. What is the person who aspires to live by the Law to do with regard to these?

The answer seems to be to internalize the values that emerge from the Torah and apply them to all our behaviors in the way that we believe best realizes those values. In the Book of Deuteronomy, Moses offers the following counsel, after repeating the mandate to keep God's commandments and statutes: "And you shall do that which is right and good in the sight of the Lord" (Deut. 6:18).

When the Torah and rabbis are silent, the guiding principle for personal behavior should therefore be what is "right and good in the sight of the Lord." That is also described in brief as "*kiddush Hashem,*" "the sanctification of God's name."

To what extent should the values of the society in which one lives fill the spaces that religious law leaves open, as the individual tries to decide how to honor God's name? In an essay on this question, our son, Rabbi Ethan Tucker of Yeshivat Mechon Hadar, cites Moses' counsel to the Israelites in Deuteronomy 4:6:

> Guard and perform [the mitzvot], for doing so is your wisdom and understanding in the eyes of the nations. When they hear all of these rules, they will say, "What a wise and understanding people is this great nation."

These verses essentially define *kiddush Hashem*. We sanctify God's name by acting ethically, according to God's Law, and thereby engender the admiration of the broader community for this Law. The behavioral standard of *kiddush Hashem* is about the third-party perception of God and the Law, based on our behavior.

Rabbi Tucker takes the discussion of what to do when the Bible and Talmud are silent a step further by quoting Rabbi Moshe Shmuel Glasner, a Hungarian rabbi of the nineteenth and twentieth centuries:

> If one violates anything that is agreed upon as abominable by enlightened people, even if it is not explicitly forbidden by the Torah, he is worse than one who violates one of the laws of the Torah.

For example, the Bible does not say, "Don't eat a sandwich that has fallen into the gutter and is covered with polluted slime." But eating such a sandwich would be offensive to any civilized person, and it is therefore prohibited as part of the "internal Torah command...to be holy." [1]

---

1. Rabbi Ethan Tucker, "Ethical Norms as the Foundation of Torah," *Parashat VaEtchanan* (Mechon Hadar Center for Jewish Law and Values, Av 5776), 3.

But what if one's idea of *kiddush Hashem* is at variance with public opinion on a particular matter? What if the societal value is not as self-evident as in the case of the defiled sandwich? What if the prevailing societal view of an act not specifically prohibited by Jewish law is inconsistent with the "internal Torah command…to be holy"? In such a case, I would recommend breaking from the societal norm and honoring God's name. Such action would represent the Jewish and Torah view of what is ultimately "right and good."

From my reading of history and my personal experience in government, I know of many sad cases where leaders were not brave enough to renounce societal norms and do the "right and the good." But I also know that the past is rich with cases of leaders who have had the courage to do what they thought was right, even when it was not popular.

Day 36

Reward and Punishment

The biblical laws are not merely precatory invocations for good behavior. They include a system of rewards and punishments that lend internal force to the specific laws and commandments. The Ten Commandments themselves contain several mentions of rewards and punishments, including the broad promise of the Second Commandment that God will show kindness to thousands of generations of those who love and obey Him. This indeed is a strong incentive to live according to the Law.

This concept of reward and punishment established a standard for all systems of law that followed. Both biblical and secular laws since then include specific penalties to dissuade people from violating them.

But when it comes to rewards for obeying the laws, the biblical and secular systems are very different. The rewards for not violating secular laws are indirect: you avoid the penalties that result from illegal behavior, and you have the satisfaction of knowing you did the right thing. In the biblical legal system, there are significant rewards for following the commandments and the law. They range from the earthly and agricultural to the messianic and eternal.

These rewards are enumerated in the Bible, with some repeated in our daily prayers. For example, twice daily, we follow the recitation of the *Shema Yisrael* declaration of monotheism from Deuteronomy chapter 6, "Hear O Israel, the Lord our God, the Lord is One" (v. 4), with a paragraph from Deuteronomy chapter 11, which delineates the biblical rewards for following the law and living by the values of the commandments:

> If you indeed heed My commandments with which I charge you today, to love the Lord your God and worship Him with all your heart and with all your soul, I will give you rain in your land in its season ... and you shall gather in your grain, wine, and oil. I will give grass in your field for your cattle, and you shall eat and be satisfied. (Vv. 13–15)

The most basic rewards for loving God and heeding His commandments are agricultural. From the time the Torah was given through the period of the two Temples in Jerusalem (and again today in modern Israel), agricultural blessings were existential blessings.

The *Shema* continues with the penalty for failing to obey God's commandments:

> Be careful lest your heart be tempted and you go astray and worship other gods ... then the Lord's anger will flare against you and He will close the heavens so that there will be no rain ... and you will perish [or, be banished] from the good land that the Lord is giving you. (Vv. 16–17)

But the Torah, and the *Keriat Shema* which quotes it, also teach how to avoid this terrible fate: by instilling the word of God in our hearts and souls, binding them on our arms and foreheads (tefillin), teaching them to our children, and writing them on our doorposts (mezuzot). The general reward for upholding God's laws in these ways is "that you and your children may live long in the land that the Lord swore to your ancestors to give them, for as long as the heavens are above the earth" (Deut. 11:21).

The prophets describe additional otherworldly rewards for following the commandments. These are embedded in the traditional prayer service in the prayer *"U'Va LeTziyon Go'el,"* "A Redeemer Will Come to Zion," recited both in the daily service and on the Sabbath and holidays:

> Blessed is our God who gave us the Torah of truth, planting within us eternal life. May it be Your will that we keep Your laws in this world, and thus be worthy to live, and inherit goodness and blessing in the Messianic Age, and in the life of the World to Come.

This uplifting vision of the rewards that will accrue to the followers of God's Law compellingly speaks to some of our most profound and perplexing questions: How should I behave? Does anyone care? What are the consequences of good and bad behavior? Is there anything after life on earth?

This dream of heavenly and eternal blessing is the Jewish people's destiny, toward which the entire Bible narrative is directed. Realizing it, however, depends on the way we behave. The kabbalists suggested that the etymology of the word "mitzva," usually translated as "commandment," is actually from the word *betzavta*, which means "together." The secret of the commandments is having a relationship with God, of walking together with God, by observing His law and doing good deeds.

Day 37

Law Enforcement

It has been said that law exists in society in proportion to its necessity. By the time the Israelites encamped at the foot of Mount Sinai, humankind had accrued a long history of misbehavior. Beginning in the Garden of Eden when Adam and Eve violated God's first law, continuing with the murder of Abel by his brother Cain, and deteriorating until God was forced to send a flood that destroyed everyone but Noah and his family, human history made the need for laws and harsh penalties abundantly clear.

Our earthly laws are intended to keep us within the straight and narrow path. Without attendant punishments, who would follow them?

Some people might obey laws simply because doing so expresses their values, and that is reason enough. "The reward for a good deed," the Mishna says, "is the deed itself" (Mishna Avot 4:2). But we cannot always rely on that inspiring standard.

Charlotte Bronte effectively made this point in her book *Jane Eyre*: "Laws and principles are not for the times when there is no temptation.

They are for such moments as this when body and soul rise in mutiny against such rigor."[1]

As a US senator, all civil or criminal laws I sponsored included a section that imposed penalties for failure to follow the law. As attorney general of Connecticut, I could not have enforced laws if they did not contain penalty clauses.

Many of the laws given by God at Sinai were accompanied by explicit penalties.[2] The Second and Third Commandments contain internal enforcement clauses. In the catalogue of "ordinances" that immediately follow the Ten Commandments in the Torah, the punishments are clearly delineated; for example, the different punishments for committing murder or manslaughter, violating the Sabbath, dishonoring parents, committing adultery, stealing property, and bearing false witness.

Although the punishments in the Torah are often harsh, Jewish sources – even the earliest rabbinic sources – teach that the toughest punishments were rarely, if ever, fully enforced. Apparently, these severe punishments are more a statement of values than a penal code, a description of what the perpetrator of the most heinous crimes deserves, but not necessarily what a human court will impose.

This is also true for what is probably the most frequently cited law enforcement principle in the Bible, "An eye for an eye." Considered within its historical context, this law as stated in the Book of Exodus could be considered criminal justice reform. "An eye for an eye" required that the punishment fit the crime, which was a far cry from the existing concepts of justice in the ancient world. By declaring that one may not kill a person who has caused another to lose an eye, or blind both eyes

---

1. Charlotte Bronte, *Jane Eyre* (London: Smith, Elder and Co., 1847), ch. 27.
2. In addition to the Ten Commandments received directly through divine revelation, the term "at Sinai" refers as well to the laws taught throughout the Books of Exodus and Leviticus, transmitted while the Jews were encamped at the foot of Mount Sinai.

of a person who had caused the loss of one eye, the Torah mapped out a radical new concept of criminal justice: proportionality.

When it came time to enforce this law, Jewish courts never allowed an "eye" to be taken at all. They opined that such a punishment, even if well deserved, might result in the death of the criminal because of the effects of removing his eye and would therefore be a disproportionate punishment and unacceptable. The aggressor was instead required to pay an appropriate monetary fine to the victim. The earthly courts meted out punishments they felt were firmly within the realm of human interaction, and left divine retribution in God's hands.[3]

In the case of premeditated murder, however, the rabbis ruled that monetary damages were inadequate. If convicted according to strict evidentiary rules, the perpetrator would be sentenced to death. Premeditated murder is an enormous desecration of God's name and God's creation.

In sum, the Sinaitic system of law includes penalties – not because God derives pleasure from man's suffering or needs to take revenge, but because these penalties are necessary if law is to be effective in bringing security, justice, and morality to human society. Therefore, when a person is sentenced to death, the Jewish court is required to choose the most respectful manner of execution.[4] The Torah and the Talmud remind us again and again to "Love your neighbor as yourself." Thus, even severe penalties are to be enforced with mercy.

---

3. See Rabbi Ari D. Kahn, "*Lex Talionis*: Law and Ethics," in *Echoes of Eden: Sefer Shmot* (Jerusalem: OU Press/Gefen Publishing House, 2012), 149–163.
4. This teaching is found multiple times in the Talmud; see, for example, Sanhedrin 45a.

Day 38

Why the Majority Rules

We believe as a matter of faith that God's Law is perfect, but we know that we humans who aspire to live by it are imperfect.

The rule of law has proven to be the best way for people to regulate and improve their behavior. Similarly, democratic legal principles – including the rule of the majority – have proven to be the best, if imperfect, way for societies to govern themselves.

And yet, rule of law societies have exonerated murderers, and democracies have elected scoundrels. In fact, even majorities on the US Supreme Court have reached decisions that seem wrong. That was surely true in the nineteenth-century case of *Plessy v. Ferguson*, which upheld race-based slavery as constitutional. It was, I believe, also true in the case of *Bush v. Gore* – a year 2000 case in which I was involved – when a five-member majority of the Supreme Court decided a national election without any basis in precedent for doing so.

The Talmud illustrates how the Sanhedrin, the Jewish Supreme Court, also struggled with the problem of human error. When the

Temple stood in Jerusalem, the Sanhedrin was invested with both legislative and judicial powers. The members of this court were the foremost legal minds of their day. Decisions were determined by majority votes. Occasionally, a majority of these highly skilled jurists made mistakes, but their decisions were nonetheless upheld.

In one particularly provocative and instructive instance, the Talmud describes how the majority of members of the court disagreed with their colleague R. Eliezer. When every argument R. Eliezer offered in support of his view was rejected, he resorted to supernatural proofs to buttress his position. Trees were uprooted, streams reversed their flow, and a voice rang out from heaven confirming R. Eliezer's opinion (Bava Metzia 59b).

Amazingly, the members of the majority held their ground, insisting that their majority view must be sustained. It made no difference to them that God supported the minority opinion; signs and wonders were irrelevant to their decision. Even the heavenly voice that spoke out in support of R. Eliezer was inadmissible. In the now-famous words of one of the judges, "[The law] is not in heaven." The adjudication of law on earth must follow procedure. It must be based on precedent and majority rule.

This talmudic account grapples with a question that continues to challenge democratic legal systems: What wins out – procedure or substance? In the case of R. Eliezer, majority rule of the court clearly prevailed over the substance of its decision – even when God Himself attested to the correctness of the minority opinion.

On the other hand, one of the commandments given by God at Sinai was, "After the majority must one incline" (Ex. 23:2). In the legal clash between R. Eliezer and the other sages, both sides of the argument could rightfully claim divine support for their view.

But how can we ignore the truth, spoken by God Himself, in favor of the mistaken opinion of the majority? The *Sefer HaḤinukh*, "The Book of Instruction," an authoritative (though anonymously authored) medieval text, grappled with this question:

…meaning even if they are mistaken in a particular ruling, it is not appropriate for us to argue with them; rather, we follow their mistake. For it is better to suffer one mistake, and to remain subject to their well-informed opinions, rather than have each and every individual act according to his own opinion, for that would cause the destruction of our religion, a division among the people, and the complete loss of the nation. It is for these reasons that the intention of the Torah was transmitted to the sages of Israel, and it was commanded that the minority would always submit to the majority. (*Sefer HaḤinukh,* mitzva 496)

The rejection of legal procedure would lead to anarchy and to legal, social, and national chaos. The author of the *Sefer HaḤinukh* argues pragmatically that it is better to suffer occasional mistakes than to risk the collapse of the entire system.[1]

And that is one reason Vice President Gore decided not to pursue the remaining option to return to the Florida Supreme Court after the decision by the US Supreme Court which he and I believed was profoundly wrong. The legitimacy of a Supreme Court majority and the continuity of our government were at stake.

---

1. A more in-depth treatment of the issues raised here can be found in Rabbi Ari D. Kahn, *Echoes of Eden: Sefer Devarim* (Jerusalem: OU Press/Gefen Publishing House, 2016), 217–228. This topic will be examined in greater depth in the forthcoming Rabbi Ari D. Kahn, *The Crowns on the Letters.*

Day 39

From God with Love

At the foundation of the world's three great monotheistic religions is the faith that God didn't merely create the world and then depart for the next challenge. Jews, Christians, and Muslims all believe that God continues to care for us as a loving parent would. In Judaism, belief in a creation that was divine and intentional is central, as is the covenant that God forged with Abraham, and the emancipation from slavery in Egypt. These are all great proofs of God's love.

But I believe that the defining act of God's love from the perspective of Judaism was the giving of the Ten Commandments and the Torah on Mount Sinai. This gift of justice, given with divine love, turned the tribes of Israel into a nation with an eternal purpose: to live by the Law and to share its values with the rest of the world through its code of conduct and system of justice. In fact, over time, about half the people on earth, most of them Christians and Muslims, became partners in the Jewish mission by embracing the values of the Ten Commandments that came forth from Sinai.

During the twelfth century, Maimonides even suggested that Christianity and Islam may be part of a divine plan to prepare the world at large for universal monotheism. In a controversial comment, he wrote:

> The thoughts of the Creator of the world are not within the power of man to reach them, for our ways are not His ways, nor are our thoughts His thoughts. And all these matters of Jesus of Nazareth and that of the Ishmaelite who arose after him are only to straighten the way of the King Messiah and to fix the entire world, to serve God as one, as it is stated: "For then I will turn the peoples [into] clear speech, to all call in the name of God and serve Him unanimously" (Zeph. 3:9). How [will this come about]? The entire world has already become filled with the mention of the Messiah, with words of Torah and words of mitzvot and these matters have spread to the furthermost isles. (*Mishneh Torah, Hilkhot Melakhim* 11:11–12)

The Jewish people have become known not as the People of Creation, or the People of the Exodus, or the People of the Holy Land, all titles that would have been appropriate. Rather, they became known as the People of the Book – the Torah, the Bible, the Ten Commandments – who have spread its messages and values to the entire world. The Law is the essence of who we Jews are and what our national purpose has always been.

Although God's Law is often demanding and difficult, God gave it to us out of love. He knew that without it we, His children, would stray, and, in the end, might well destroy ourselves. With it, we have a chance to improve our lives and our societies.

And we have.

Day 40

A Senate Sermon

During the summer of 1963, between my junior and senior years at college, I worked as an intern for US Senator Abraham Ribicoff, former governor of Connecticut and member of the Kennedy cabinet. He was a hero to me, and an inspiration for my public service.

One day, Senator Ribicoff called me into his office. That, in itself, was exciting. He told me that he had been invited by one of the titans of the Senate (I believe it was Senator Richard Russell of Georgia) to address the prayer breakfast at which Christian senators gathered weekly. Senator Ribicoff was Jewish but not religiously observant. He knew that I was religious, and asked if I would draft remarks for him to deliver at the prayer breakfast on the subject his colleagues had asked him to address: "Is the God of the Old Testament a God of Vengeance?"

The remarks I prepared argued that the God of the Old Testament was not a God of vengeance, but a loving father who sets standards of behavior for His children and chastises them when they fail to meet those standards. He never abandons them and always judges them with mercy. God's acts of love toward humanity are enormous – including giving the Ten Commandments to bring order, justice, and morality into human existence. As members of the Senate knew from their own work of legislating, I added, the law must often be strict, but only because that is necessary to achieve larger societal purposes.

After the prayer breakfast, when Senator Ribicoff returned to his office, he called me in. He said that his remarks had been well received by his colleagues, which, he thought, would positively affect his ability, as a freshman senator, to work with them.

The senator's words have stayed with me. And so have my views about God as a loving Father and His Law as necessary and constructive for His children.

Day 41

Lawyer Jokes and Serious Laws

Lawyer jokes – or more accurately, anti-lawyer jokes – are a staple of American humor. Here is an example:

> A doctor, an engineer, and a lawyer got into a debate about whose profession was the oldest. The doctor said it was his because there must have been a doctor in the Garden of Eden to help God make Adam's rib into Eve. Oh no, the engineer argued, before that there must have been an engineer who assisted God in transforming primordial chaos into the order of the universe. Obviously, the lawyer concluded, you were both late. There must have been a lawyer there to create the chaos.

One of the few tests of my wonderful friendship with my former Senate colleague John McCain is that I have had to listen to him tell the identical lawyer joke at least fifty times. And I have surprised myself by laughing every time.

Even the British J. K. Rowling got into the act in *Harry Potter and the Deathly Hallows*: "Are you planning to follow a career in Magical Law, Miss Granger?" asked Scrimgeour. "No, I'm not," retorted Hermione, "I'm hoping to do some good in the world."

Unfortunately, some lawyers behave in a way that justifies these barbs. The system, however, in which lawyers normally play so critical and constructive a part in adjudicating rights and wrongs and peacefully settling disputes is one of the greatest assets of rule of law societies like America and Israel. It all began at Sinai, when God gave the Law to the Children of Israel.

In rule of law countries, individuals know they can rely on the justice system to punish those who have wronged them. There is no need for extralegal vigilante action to achieve justice. Businesses know the courts will fairly resolve commercial disputes and protect them from lawless expropriation of their property by the government. In fact, these considerations are among the major reasons why American and international businesses prefer to invest in countries like America, where there is rule of law, and why they are reluctant to invest in countries without an independent and reliable justice system.

In *Ethics of the Fathers*, the sages warned that those who practice law must be especially careful not to be involved in any endeavor that creates a miscarriage of justice (Mishna Avot 1:8). The Talmud teaches that the jurist who rules in a true and just manner becomes a partner with God in the act of creation (Shabbat 10a), because without law, the world would revert to the chaos that existed before Creation.

I was once with another great friend from the Senate, Lindsey Graham, when we were introduced to a young law student. "It's really great to meet you," Lindsey said, "because the world is one more lawyer short of perfection and you could be it."

Section Five

Shavuot, Celebrating the Law

Day 42

The Law and Cheesecake

I love Shavuot, not only because of what we celebrate, but also because of how and when we celebrate. First, the holiday occurs at a beautiful time of year – in May or June. To honor both the springtime and the agricultural origin of the holiday, most synagogues and many homes are decorated with plants and flowers. This custom also reflects the midrashic understanding that flowers burst forth from Mount Sinai just before the giving of the Ten Commandments and the Torah.

Second, there is the opportunity (rarely afforded to people after they leave university) to stay up all night studying – but not to cram for a final exam. Rather, it is to study the Torah and hear the epochal events at Sinai, including the giving and accepting of the Ten Commandments, read from the Torah at the morning service. For those who stay up all night studying, the morning service begins as the sun rises. For me, this is a stirring spiritual experience. And, on top of all that, I love Shavuot because it is a short holiday, that allows us to get back to work after only one day in Israel, and two days in the Diaspora.

Another unique Shavuot custom I especially enjoy is the focus on dairy foods. Many reasons for this custom are given. In fact, one author collected 150 reasons for eating dairy on Shavuot, which suggests that the custom may have no definitive rationale. It is, as Sholom Aleichem's Tevye the Milkman would say, "tradition."

As a long-time legislator, who heard appeals for help from various economic interest groups, I once imagined that the custom was the brainchild of an Association of Jewish Dairy Farmers who complained to the rabbis that it was unfair that on the Sabbath and all of the Jewish holidays the custom was to eat meat. Couldn't at least one holiday feature dairy products?

My favorite serious explanation, however, goes back to the Middle Ages, when children were initiated into the world of Torah study with sweet treats to make their first taste of learning positive. This custom was based on the verse from the Song of Songs, "Sweetness drops from your lips, O bride; honey and milk are under your tongue" (Song. 4:11), which was interpreted as a metaphor for the Jewish people's love of Torah. On Shavuot, the day we celebrate receiving the Torah, the idea of "honey and milk under your tongue" is expressed literally, in unique culinary customs. Over time, the traditional honey and milk took on new – and delicious – forms, in cheesecakes, cheese blintzes, etc.

Thank God for anti-cholesterol medication.

Day 43

Shavuot Highlights

The high point of the observance of Shavuot for me, and, for many others, I imagine, comes at the morning service. The Torah scrolls – still crafted, as they have always been, from animal skin parchment with the holy words still penned by quill – are taken from the ark, carried around the congregation, kissed by the congregants, and then placed on the *bima* or central table. The scrolls are opened to the Book of Exodus and the chapter describing the arrival of Moses and the Israelites at Mount Sinai and the receiving of the Ten Commandments from God is read.

The sages taught that, on Passover, we must see ourselves as if we personally experienced the Exodus from Egypt. On Shavuot, the rabbis say, we *were* all there at Mount Sinai, in some metaphysical sense, to accept the Ten Commandments and Torah. They were offered to each and every one of us – not just to the people who were physically present, or to a religious, economic, or political elite – then, now, and forever.

On Shavuot morning, in Ashkenazic synagogues, everyone stands silently as the Ten Commandments are read aloud. At the Exodus of the

Israelites from Egypt, God kept His promises to Abraham, made generations earlier. At Sinai, the covenant was renewed in another exchange of legal promises, another contract, this one between God and all of Israel for all time. And this time, the covenant was broadened and deepened by God's laws and their acceptance by the Israelites. On the morning of Shavuot, as we stand and listen to the Ten Commandments, it is as if we are renewing the vows the Israelites exchanged with God on that morning more than three thousand years ago at Mount Sinai, when they said "*naase venishma*," "we will do and we will obey."

Our renewal of the covenant follows the *Tikkun Leil Shavuot* – the intense night-long learning of the Law – a title that can be translated as "improving the night of Shavuot."

We discussed the phrase "*tikkun olam*," a concise, but all-encompassing, way to describe the purpose of Judaism in improving or repairing the world. The *Tikkun Leil Shavuot* is also about improvement. This tradition originated with the kabbalists. Rabbi Yosef Karo and Rabbi Shlomo Alkabetz stayed up one Shavuot night learning Torah. When they later moved to Safed, Israel, their custom became widespread.[1] They called it a "*Tikkun*," which according to the kabbalists, represents a spiritual correction for a mistake or failing.

In this case, the correction was thought to be required for the behavior of the Children of Israel who, according to the Midrash, overslept on the morning the Ten Commandments were to be given. God was forced to sound the heavenly shofar to awaken them, and as redress for this terrible behavior, the kabbalists taught, we should stay up the whole night of Shavuot to make sure we would be awake at dawn to receive the Ten Commandments.

I have appreciated the *Tikkun Leil Shavuot* more as the years have gone by. When I was younger, I would usually drop into a study

---

1. R. J. Zwi Werblowsky, *Joseph Karo: Lawyer and Mystic* (Oxford: Oxford Press, 1962), 211.

session at my synagogue or at the Hillel at Yale, or I would study on my own at home. When my wife, Hadassah, and I settled in the Westville section of New Haven, we had a wonderful group of religiously observant neighbors who would meet every Shabbat afternoon to study and discuss the Torah portion we had read that morning in synagogue. On the night of Shavuot, we convened a *Tikkun* in a different house every year. Though it didn't usually go past midnight, our study sessions were full of stimulating conversation – and great dairy desserts.

In 2007, Hadassah and I moved back to Stamford (to be closer to our children in New York) and we rejoined my original congregation, Agudath Sholom. There, on Shavuot, we participated in some thoughtful and provocative discussions that continued all night, spiritually moving morning services, and breakfasts, which I can only describe as haute cuisine, prepared for the whole congregation by two wonderful fellow congregants, Mitch and Susan Mailman.

My most memorable *Tikkun* was in 2015, when our family observed Shavuot in Israel. I spent the holiday night at Yeshivat Netiv Aryeh in Jerusalem, where the view is directly to the Kotel, the remaining western wall of the Temple complex. The *Tikkun* comprised a brilliant and wide-ranging learning session conducted by Rabbi Aharon Bina, the head of the yeshiva. I spent the night learning with my son-in-law, Dr. Daniel Lowenstein, who had studied at Netiv Aryeh years earlier, and my friend, Ira Rennert, a generous supporter of the yeshiva. The night passed quickly; never were we even tempted by sleep. At dawn, we prayed the morning prayers. We reaccepted the Ten Commandments as the sun rose over the Kotel and the nearby plaza, which had filled with tens of thousands of worshipers.

Day 44

A Mystical Shavuot

Since I touched on Kabbala in the previous essay, I will share with you a mystical experience I had years ago on Shavuot, which affected the rest of my life. I was raised in an Orthodox Jewish home. When I left for college, I dropped some but not all of my observance of the laws and customs. For example, I continued to pray every morning but I stopped observing the Sabbath and the Jewish festivals – Passover, Shavuot, and Sukkot.

In 1967, my grandmother, who was a very religious woman and a major force in my life, died. And my first son was born. That cycle of one family generation ending and a new one beginning raised in me the question of whether I would be the conduit through which my grand-mother's faith and observance would pass on to my children, or let it all end. I chose to carry it forward, returning step-by-step to observance of the Sabbath, the festivals, and more.

By the early 1970s, I was fully observing Shabbat, but on the festivals, after attending services in the synagogue in the morning, and sharing a meal with my family, I would go to work in the afternoon. After I had become a state senator, I committed to a political event during the afternoon of one Shavuot holiday. I was feeling guilty about doing so, but I did not want to back out of my commitment.

When I closed the front door of my house as I left for the event, something flew by my eyes. I looked down at the stoop and saw a *klaf*, the small piece of parchment that sits inside the mezuza, which Jews are commanded to put on their doorposts. Written on the *klaf* are the monotheistic declaration, "Hear O Israel, the Lord our God, the Lord is One," and then the two paragraphs of the *Keriat Shema* that follow, which observant Jews recite, as part of the morning and evening services, each day. These paragraphs contain the essential commands to love the Lord our God and serve Him with all our heart, soul, and might. If we do, we are promised to live well and forever on the land; if we don't, we won't. As part of our service of God, we are to put on tefillin every day, place mezuzot on our doorposts, and teach the commandments to our children. Going to a political event on Shavuot was in direct violation of those commandments.

I looked at my front doorpost and, sure enough, the back of the mezuza had come loose, releasing the *klaf* to the ground. I had opened and shut that door any number of times. Why did it now unsettle the mezuza?

For me, the answer was clear. I looked up and said: "OK, God. I got the message. This is the last time I go to a political event or work on one of the festivals." And it was.

I could not be happier about that decision.

Ruth, a Love Story and an Allegory

Most Jewish communities read the Book of Ruth during morning services on Shavuot. A beautiful, romantic story, it fittingly reflects the rabbinic view that the giving of the Ten Commandments and their acceptance was like a marriage ceremony between God and the Israelites.

The Book of Ruth begins with a man named Elimelekh, who, when famine strikes Israel, uproots his family from their hometown of Bethlehem and leaves his country and people behind.

The names of the characters and places in the book of Ruth are instructive, indicative even of divine justice. Elimelekh leaves behind the city of Bethlehem – Hebrew for "house of bread." Ironically, as the story opens, there is no *leḥem*, "bread," in Bethlehem. According to the Midrash, Elimelekh, who was wealthy, apparently abandoned his town to protect his fortune from the appeals of suffering neighbors. He takes his wife, his sons, and his wealth to the Plains of Moab. Soon afterward, Elimelekh dies; his sons Mahlon, a name meaning "diseased one," and Kilion, "eradicated one," marry Moabite women, and they too die.

Elimelekh's widow, Naomi, decides to return to Israel. Initially, both of Naomi's daughters-in-law offer to return with her, but Naomi presents them with the harsh realities that argue against their kind proposals. Orpah, which means "nape of the neck," relents and returns to her father's house in Moab. But Ruth is not swayed by Naomi's attempts to convince her to stay in Moab as well. She declares in beautiful, now famous words:

> Do not entreat me to leave you. Wherever you go I will go…your people is my people, and your God is my God. Where you die, I will die, and there I will be buried. So may the Lord do to me and so may He continue, for nothing but death will separate me from you. (Ruth 1:16–17)

Ruth's devotion is absolute as she accompanies her elderly, now impoverished mother-in-law to a strange new land. Ruth also embodies loyalty and kindness, the very traits Elimelekh and his sons lacked.

Back in Bethlehem, Boaz, a relative of Elimelekh, notices Ruth collecting stray stalks of wheat in his fields, as poor people were permitted to do. He is impressed by Ruth's demeanor and respect for Jewish customs. He asks about her and learns that this young immigrant from a foreign land has taken it upon herself to care for her mother-in-law, Naomi. Instead of xenophobically rejecting Ruth, or gloating over the downfall of Elimelekh's household, Boaz instructs his workers to look out for this "stranger" and be sure that she, and Naomi, have plenty of food. He warns his field hands that she must not be harmed or molested in any way.

In an ironic reversal, Ruth is extended the support and protection of a wealthy landowner willing to assume the role shunned by Elimelekh.

Boaz is a man of principle, and he rewards Ruth for the kindness she has shown Naomi.

The Book of Ruth is ultimately the story of those who embrace and embody the values of the Torah and the Ten Commandments, represented by Ruth, who chooses to adopt Jewish law and values, and Boaz, who reflects the best social justice values received at Sinai. In the end, Boaz marries Ruth and they (and Naomi) live happily ever after. In fact, they merit to establish the Kingdom of the House of David, through their great-grandson David who, according to tradition, was born and died on Shavuot.

Over the centuries, several reasons have been given for reading the Book of Ruth on Shavuot. One of the most obvious is that the story of Ruth occurs in an agricultural setting at harvest time, as does the counting of the Omer, and the celebration of the First Fruits on Shavuot.

Another explanation is that the Book of Ruth is an allegory for acceptance of the Ten Commandments and Torah by the Israelites at Sinai, and the fulfillment of the covenant between Abraham and God. On Shavuot at Sinai, the Israelites accepted the Torah and became the Jewish nation, just as Ruth chose to join the Jewish people and accept their laws and values.

Today, when controversy about what constitutes a valid conversion to Judaism abounds, I will not be the first or last to note that Ruth's conversion seems to be based on the simple, sincere declaration: "Your people is my people, and your God is my God."

I believe that the most important reason why Ruth is read on Shavuot is to remind us that the religion that Ruth accepted is about the values of love, honor, and kindness that are the essence of the Law given at Sinai. The Law can be stern, mechanical, and dry, but the values it aims to spread are as personal, emotional, and compelling as the Book of Ruth.

Day 46

Returning to the Land

The Bible mandates that when the Jewish people enter the Promised Land, they are to count the days between Passover and Shavuot, but only then, because Passover and Shavuot and the days between them are firmly rooted in the agricultural cycle of the Land of Israel.

The agricultural aspect of these holidays, related to the Land of Israel, is amplified by the Torah's other names for them. Passover is called Ḥag HaAviv, "the Festival of Spring," and Shavuot is called Ḥag HaBikkurim, "the Festival of the First Fruits." Each year, in the period of Sefirat HaOmer, "counting the Omer," we are counting the days and weeks from the start of spring – Ḥag HaAviv – until the time the first fruits ripen fifty days later, on Ḥag HaBikkurim. On that festival, the ancient Israelites carried the fruits of their labors to the Temple in Jerusalem, and gave thanks for their God-given bounty.

These agricultural elements of Shavuot are temporally consistent with the earlier historical events that transpired on these days: the Exodus from Egypt to freedom, followed by the Divine Revelation at Sinai. Shavuot joins the joy and beauty of nature's rebirth to these two foundational events of Jewish history, and enables us to celebrate them all together.

In the generations of Jewish exile from the Land of Israel, the agricultural aspects of the festivals naturally took a back seat to the historical aspects. However, with the rebirth of the modern Jewish State of Israel, Israeli farmers renewed their love affair with the land and reconnected with the agricultural aspect of the festivals. Even many secular Israeli kibbutzim, collective agricultural communities, began to celebrate Shavuot, the Festival of the First Fruits, reenacting the ancient practice of *Bikkurim* and returning the holiday to its biblical roots.

Day 47

Reframing the Omer

A familiar joke goes: "Tell me in brief about the Jewish holidays."

"OK. They tried to kill us. God saved us. Let's eat."

Shavuot does not fit the pattern, except for the eating. It is all about gratitude and joy. The seven weeks of counting the Omer between Passover and Shavuot should also be. But, as if to bring life into line with the joke, Jewish tradition, since ancient times, has incorporated an element of sadness and semi-mourning into the days of the Omer to commemorate a plague that struck the students of Rabbi Akiva almost two thousand years ago, killing 24,000 of them. This happened during the Israelite revolt, led by Bar Kokhba, against the Romans in the years 132–136. Since Rabbi Akiva supported Bar Kokhba, there is a widely held belief that his students were killed by the Romans in retaliation or in combat. As a result, many observant Jews maintain mourning practices such as not cutting their hair, shaving, listening to music, or holding weddings or parties for a thirty-three-day period during the Omer count.

I honor the memory of those students of Rabbi Akiva who died fighting alongside Bar Kokhba for their freedom. But the clouds of mourning which perhaps sometimes hover too thickly over the days of the Omer should not completely obscure the underlying festive nature of the period as days to be filled with gratitude, rising expectations, and joyous study of the Law.

By focusing on the festive aspect of the Omer period, we would be following in the footsteps of Rabbi Akiva himself. His capacity to persevere in the worst of times, and to do so with supreme optimism, distinguished him as the "greatest of the rabbis." A talmudic story told about Rabbi Akiva underscores this quality. After the Temple was destroyed, Rabbi Akiva and a few of his colleagues were walking on Mount Scopus in Jerusalem overlooking the site of the Temple. They saw a fox scurry from under the ruins of what had been the Holy of Holies, the most sacred inner sanctum of the Temple. Rabbi Akiva's colleagues, overcome by hopelessness, began to weep. Rabbi Akiva began to laugh. Astonished, they asked him how he could laugh at a moment framed in such utter despair. Rabbi Akiva answered:

> The fulfillment of the prophecy that Jerusalem will be destroyed and desolate is the greatest proof that another prophecy about Jerusalem will also one day be fulfilled. That is the prophecy, "Old men and old women shall yet again dwell in the streets of Jerusalem."

Rabbi Akiva was able to see, in the midst of destruction, the seeds of redemption.

In fact, as Rabbi Akiva foresaw, such miracles have occurred in our time and they have occurred during the Omer:

On the twentieth day of the Omer in 1948, the State of Israel declared its independence.

On the forty-second and forty-third days of the Omer in 1967, the Israel Defense Forces liberated Jerusalem, uniting, for the first time in two millennia, the religious and political capitals of the Jewish people.

On the morning of 6 Sivan 5727, Shavuot 1967, one week after Jerusalem was reunited, a crowd estimated at twenty thousand streamed through the streets and alleys at daybreak, and gathered in prayer at the Kotel. Religious and secular Jews, shoulder to shoulder, celebrated the ancient holiday of Shavuot in their newly liberated capital, in a moment of unity that was perhaps equaled only by the experience of the Israelites at Sinai.

Thanks to God and visionary, heroic men and women, there is much to be grateful for and celebrate during the time between Passover and Shavuot.

Day 48

Doing and Obeying

The sages called Shavuot *Zeman Matan Torateinu*, which means "the time of the giving of our Torah." This name focuses on the *giving*, not the *receiving*, of the Law, because what is significant and transformational about Shavuot is that God gave the Law, and spoke to the people at Sinai.

A few chapters after the Revelation, however, Moses spoke to the people, and they answered: "[Moses] took the Book of the Covenant and read it aloud to the people. They replied, 'All that God has declared, we will do and obey'" (Ex. 24:7). The Jewish people embraced the word of God in an expression of total acceptance and complete faith.

But what precisely did they embrace? Torah scholars from the time of the Talmud through the medieval period have disagreed about this. The most prominent approach is the one propounded by Rashi, whose commentary draws upon a well-known talmudic tradition that frames the statement, "We will do and obey," as primarily forward directed.[1] The Children of Israel expressed the willingness to accept the entire corpus of Jewish law, even though they had not yet heard what it would entail. In this view, the statement, "We will do and obey," represents a leap of faith. The Jewish people knew that the Giver of the Law had brought them to this point, and this was reason enough for them to accept, faithfully, His as-yet unrevealed system of law.

Nahmanides has a different opinion. Regarding the declaration, "We will do and obey," he voices several concerns. The first is that by this point in the biblical text (the twenty-fourth chapter of the Book of Exodus), four weighty chapters of law have been taught, including the Ten Commandments and the section known as *mishpatim*, literally "judgments," which outline much of civil law. Thus, Nahmanides argues that the declaration of acceptance must be read in the context of the full verse: "*All that God has [already] declared, we will do and obey.*" With this statement, the Jewish people accepted upon themselves all the laws they had already been taught by God Himself, as well as those heard by Moses on the mountain and taught to them.[2]

A third approach to the covenantal declaration of "We will do and obey" is found in the commentary known as *Ḥizkuni*, a thirteenth-century French commentator. It posits that the word of God accepted by the people as the basis for the covenantal relationship is referred to at the end of the Book of Leviticus: "These are the words and the laws taught to Moses at Sinai" (Lev. 27:34).[3] These "words and laws" include not only the laws, but the sanctions and punishments, including exile, for breaking the law, that are detailed in the Book of Leviticus.

---

1. This opinion is very similar to the earlier opinion of R. Yosi b. Yehuda in Shabbat 88a.
2. This opinion may be traced back to R. Judah the Prince (also known as "Rebbi") in *Mekhilta Yitro, Masekhta DeBeḤodesh, parasha* 3.
3. This approach may be traced back to R. Ishmael, a sage who lived hundreds of years earlier, in the *Mekhilta* above.

These three opinions regarding the acceptance of the Torah reflect three different views of Shavuot. Was receiving the Torah an act of faith? Was the acceptance based upon eyes-wide-open knowledge of part of the law, and with full understanding of the obligations it encompassed? Or was the acceptance the result of "full disclosure," of having seen the contract in its entirety, including the fine print that spelled out the consequences of lawlessness?

We are free to choose. If we prefer to experience Shavuot as a romantic rendezvous in the desert, we can accept Rashi's understanding of "We will do and obey." If we see the holiday as a celebration of the transformation of the Jewish people through the acceptance of the Law, we will favor Nahmanides' approach. And if we view Shavuot as a celebration of the signing of a contract between God and the Jewish people, with all its terms and consequences, we will adopt the approach of Ḥizkuni.

Each person's experience of the holiday of Shavuot will be shaped by his or her individual background, perspective, and temperament. We will ultimately adopt different interpretations of the covenant between God and the Jewish people that was sealed on Shavuot. But as we prepare to welcome the festival, we are joined together by the shared feelings of joy and gratitude, which are its hallmarks.

Day 49

The Laws of Sevens

Seven is a significant number in the Bible. After six days of labor, we must rest on the seventh day. There are seven weeks between Passover and Shavuot. The land rests in the Sabbatical or seventh year and the Jubilee comes after seven times seven or forty-nine years.

Chapter 25 in the Book of Leviticus details the laws of the Sabbatical year, in which the farmer is commanded to let the land lie fallow, to remind him, and all of us, that the true owner of the land is God. The agricultural theme identified with the holidays is thus expanded from the weekly and yearly cycle of celebrations to a longer time frame:

> But in the seventh year the land shall have a sabbath of complete rest, a sabbath to God: you shall not sow your field or prune your vineyard.... You shall count off seven weeks of years – seven times seven years – so that the period of seven weeks of years gives you a total of forty-nine years. Then you shall sound the shofar (horn) loud; in the seventh month, on the tenth day

of the month – the Day of Atonement – the shofar shall be sounded throughout your land and you shall hallow the fiftieth year. You shall proclaim freedom throughout the land for all its inhabitants. It shall be a jubilee for you: each of you shall return to his ancestral inheritance and each of you shall return to his family. (Lev. 25:8–13)

Interestingly, this "macro" cycle also mirrors the "micro" cycle of the counting of the Omer. The relationship between the two systems is suggested by the name given to the fiftieth year, "Jubilee" – or *Yovel* in Hebrew. *Yovel* means shofar, and it appears in only two places in the Torah: in the description of the Revelation at Mount Sinai (Ex. 19:13) and in this passage, about Yom Kippur of the Jubilee year.

The lessons of the fiftieth day after Passover (Shavuot) and the fiftieth year (Jubilee) are the same. Not only was the shofar sounded, but the purpose of blowing the shofar was the same – to declare freedom. As we have seen, the final step of the Israelites' liberation from slavery was receiving the Law at Sinai – on the fiftieth day. During the Jubilee year, lands were to return to their ancestral owners, slaves were to be set free, and debts were to be canceled. This national celebration of freedom and social justice was heralded by the sound of the shofar, the *yovel*.

In 1752, more than two decades before American independence, the Pennsylvania Provincial Assembly commissioned a large copper and tin bell in celebration of the fiftieth anniversary of Philadelphia's state constitution, a seminal declaration of human rights, itself greatly influenced by the Law from Sinai. The bell was engraved with this verse from the Book of Leviticus: "Proclaim liberty throughout all the land unto all the inhabitants thereof" (25:10). This inscription on the first iconic symbol of American freedom highlights how deeply the early Americans drew from the Hebrew Bible. When the Liberty Bell – the modern embodiment of the biblical shofar – rang out, it too proclaimed liberty and social justice throughout the land.

The first chief rabbi of modern Israel, Rabbi Abraham Isaac Kook, spoke at Independence Hall in Philadelphia on June 22, 1924. He commented that liberty is so important that one may have to work as long as forty-nine years to achieve it. This is true for individuals, as well as for nations. We pray for the day when the sound of freedom through law – the *yovel* – rings out for all peoples, wherever they may be.

Day 50

The Transformative Power of Torah Learning

I introduced this book with the objective of turning the observance of the Passover Seder from a one-night experience into a seven-week journey of study that culminates in the celebration of Shavuot. The study of Torah not only educates, it transforms. Torah study is more than an intellectual experience. It is part of a dialogue with God. When we pray, we speak to God, and when we study the Bible, we listen to what God has said. Through Torah study, the Revelation at Sinai, which took place thousands of years ago on Shavuot, continues. This contributes to an emotional experience, which contains elements of the spiritual and mystical.

Rabbi Joseph Soloveitchik once confided to a group of his students: "When I learn Torah, I feel the breath of eternity on my face." When he studied the Torah, he added, he felt as if he were in conversation with the great sages of previous generations. Torah study connects us with our past and our future, in a chain that joins millennia. The authentic Jewish culture that has stood the test of time is centered around ideas and writings that emerged from our collective learning of Torah law and values. We can help sustain Jewish continuity by making our Passover to Shavuot experience the model for a weekly or even daily encounter in which we stimulate our children to ask us questions about the Torah and the Ten Commandments.

Throughout our history, particularly during the years in exile, it was the study of Torah that allowed Jews in far-flung lands to maintain their identity and sense of community. Throughout the ages, despite their geographic separation, despite the independent nature of the communities they formed around the world, Jews shared a common heritage and destiny in the Torah, whether in the biblical text itself, the talmudic explication of the text, or later commentaries on it.

Through their study of Torah, Jews have shared a common language. They have pondered the same questions, analyzed the same comments, and considered the same solutions. A question raised in France in the 1200s might have been answered in Spain one hundred years later. A rabbi living in Yemen felt perfectly at home reading an Eastern European gloss of the Talmud. Today, a question of Jewish law raised over the internet by a student in Detroit, for example, will be answered within minutes just as easily by people from the United States, or Israel, or South Africa.

In 1923, the Orthodox Jewish organization Agudath Israel initiated worldwide study of one daily page of Talmud called *daf yomi*. Today, hundreds of thousands of Jews, men and women – most of whom are neither yeshiva students nor rabbis – participate in these learning programs. Focusing on the same page, drawing on the same reservoir of Jewish thought, they are joined into a vast community that spans continents and generations. There are additional opportunities for Torah learning offered by every Jewish denomination, Bible study sponsored by Christian groups, and more Torah and Talmud texts published in more languages than ever before.

If you have read the daily essays in this book, you have joined the community of learners across the globe who are keeping the torch of the Revelation lit, and carrying it forward. I hope you will continue to do so. Just as Passover should not be the beginning and end of one's Jewish holiday experience, a concise book like this should not be the end of your study of God's Law and values. I hope it will lead to further learning and living with the Law, uniting you with all those who strive to follow God's commandments, given at Sinai on Shavuot.

OU Press
Books that educate, inspire, enrich, and enlighten

Maggid Books
The best of contemporary Jewish thought from
Koren Publishers Jerusalem Ltd.